SUSTAINABLE
Residential Architecture

SUSTAINABLE
Residential Architecture

Ana M. Álvarez

FIREFLY BOOKS

A Firefly Book

Published by Firefly Books Ltd. 2014

First printing

Publisher Cataloging-in-Publication Data (U.S.)

A CIP record for this title is available from the Library of Congress

Library and Archives Canada Cataloguing in Publication

Álvarez, Ana María, 1976-, author
 Sustainable residential architecture / Ana M. Álvarez.
 ISBN 978-1-77085-447-5 (bound)
 1. Sustainable architecture. 2. Sustainable architecture— Designs
and plans. 3. Sustainable living. 4. Architecture, Domestic. 5.
Architecture, Domestic—Designs and plans. I. Title.
NA2542.36.A48 2014 720'.47 C2014-902877-6

Published in the United States by
Firefly Books (U.S.) Inc.
P.O. Box 1338, Ellicott Station
Buffalo, New York 14205

Published in Canada by
Firefly Books Ltd.
50 Staples Avenue, Unit 1
Richmond Hill, Ontario L4B 0A7

Printed in China

Editorial coordination: Claudia
Martínez Alonso; Art direction:
Mireia Casanovas Soley; Layout:
Cristina Simó Perales; Cover
layout: Emma Termes Parera;
Translation: Cillero & de Motta

In residential architecture today, there are more and more options for decreasing the ecological impact of home building and maintaining, and for increasing the energy efficiency and overall sustainability of the project. There are many associations and groups, such as the Association for Environment Conscious Building (AECB) and the Green Planet Architects (GPA), which offer guidance and information on the topic. With concepts such as prefabrication, modulation, innovative materials, adaptation, mobility and off-grid living, eco-architecture has reached a point at which comfort and style need not be relinquished.

The projects featured in this book, representing firms from around the globe, are examples of prefabricated (partial or total), adaptable homes with rapid assembly on-site. With prefabricated construction there is a considerable reduction in the total cost of the house (both in the construction and maintenance). The logic behind these new methods is that time and cost is saved if similar construction tasks can be carried out in a factory, so that assembly line techniques can be employed at a location where skilled tradesmen are constantly available; thus congestion at the final assembly site, which wastes time, can also be greatly reduced. The method finds application particularly where the structure is composed of repeating units or forms, or where multiple copies of the same basic structure are being constructed. Finally, other restricting conditions such as a lack of power, lack of water, exposure to harsh weather or a hazardous environment are avoided.

Throughout the book, the surface area, number of main rooms and construction methods are provided with the aim of highlighting the qualities of the project. At the back of the book you will find a directory of architects, manufacturers and builders around the world, experts in the exciting field of sustainable architecture.

Infiniski
Manifesto

Curacaví, Chile

James&Mau
www.jamesandmau.com
© Antonio Corcuera

In situ assembly, steel shipping
containers, veneer modules,
cellulose and natural cork
insulation

1,722 sq ft (160 sq m)
4 bedrooms, 3 washrooms

Of the materials used, 85 percent are
recycled, recovered and non-pollutant
products such as recycled galvanized
steel or reused laurel wood. The
structure consists of three containers;
one of them is divided in two and serves
as the structural support. A ventilated
solar film regulates temperature.

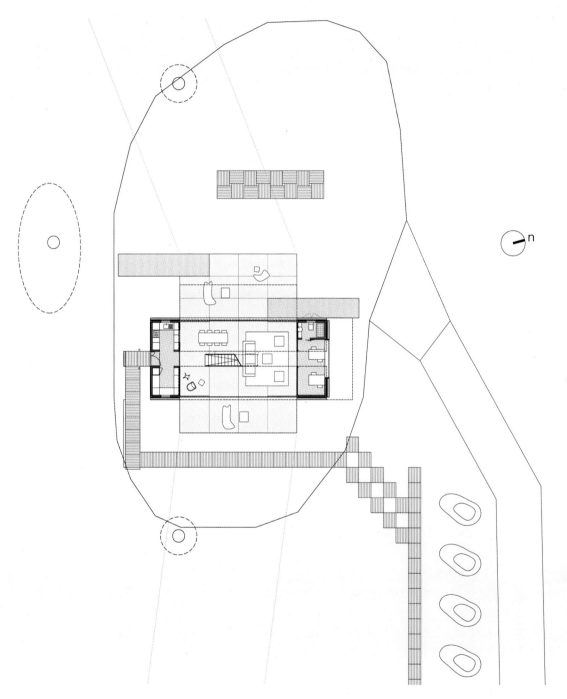

Ground floor

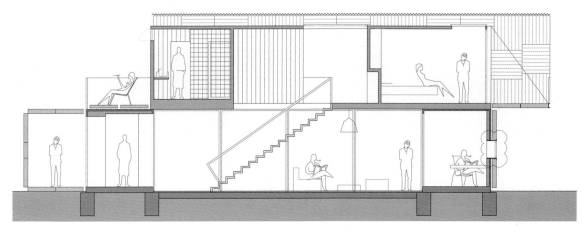

Longitudinal section

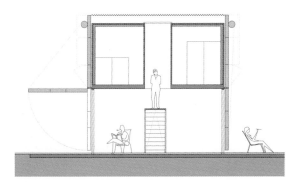

Transversal section

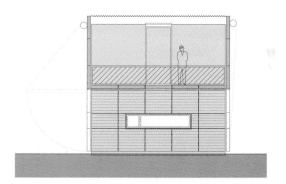

Elevation

The pergolas can be repositioned according to the season to create cool air or the effect of passive warming.

Vermont Cabin

Jamaica, Vermont, USA

Resolution: 4 Architecture
www.re4a.com
© Resolution: 4 Architecture

1,646 sq ft (153 sq m)
2 bedrooms, 2 washrooms

In situ assembly, prefabricated
wooden structure, corrugated
COR-TEN panel walls, bamboo
flooring

Isolated in an open area of the Green
Mountains, this prefabricated home is a
refuge for a couple from Brooklyn. There
is no telephone or mobile phone coverage
for this off-the-grid construction. The
floors are bamboo and have a radiant
heating system.

Electricity is generated by 3,000 kWh solar panels located a few feet from the house.

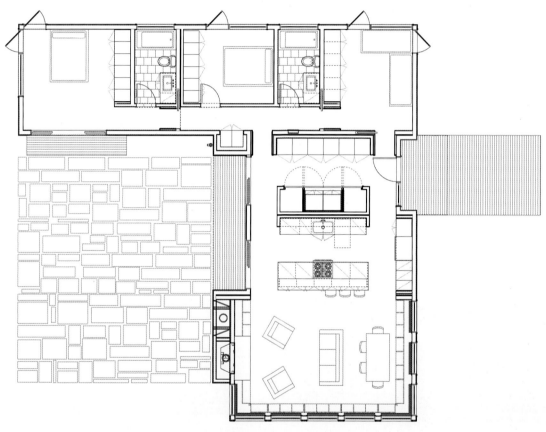

Floor plan

Watershed

Wren, Oregon, USA

FLOAT Architectural Research
and Design
www.floatwork.com
© Gary Tarleton

70 sq ft (6.5 sq m)
1 bedroom

In situ assembly, concrete pillars,
steel structure, wood panels,
glass, polycarbonate roof

The project consists of a concrete base
that supports the weight and allows
water drainage from the steel structure
that forms the frame. The wood paneling
is assembled with stainless steel screws.
The pieces can be changed, recycled or
moved separately.

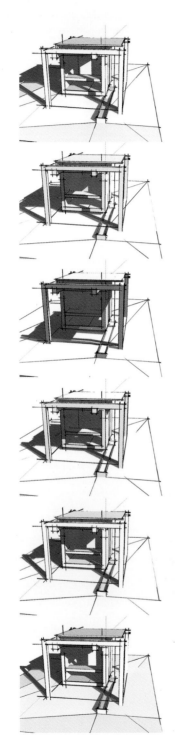
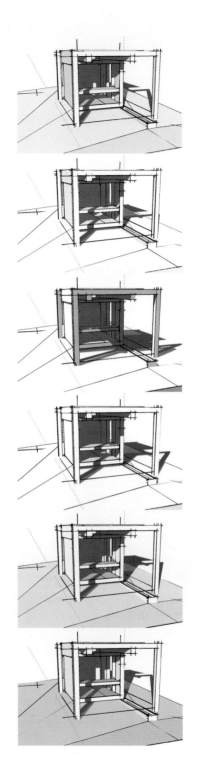

Structure details

The building process causes the least possible impact on the environment: no roads, no electricity and no land excavation.

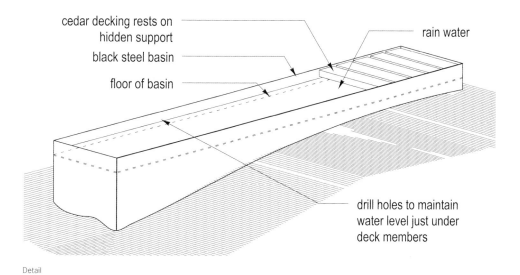

cedar decking rests on
hidden support

rain water

black steel basin

floor of basin

drill holes to maintain
water level just under
deck members

Detail

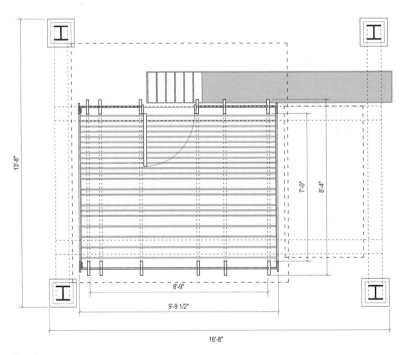

Floor plan

Evolutiv 1

Suitable for any location

Olgga Architectes
www.olgga.fr
© Patrick Blanc, Pauline Turmel

753 sq ft (70 sq m)
2 bedrooms, 2 washrooms

Factory pre-assembled modules,
in situ assembly, structure and
enclosure in chestnut

The objective of this project is to
achieve affordable housing, through
prefabricated wooden modules that are
arranged in different ways and form
different indoor and outdoor spaces.
Two or more modules can be combined,
the support system can be changed and
a green roof can be added.

The advantages of this house are the low power consumption, flexibility in the layout and provision and use of natural materials.

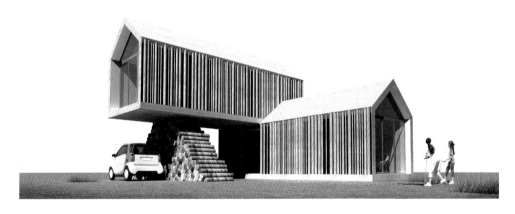

sleeping

storage box

wood heap

living

Axonometry

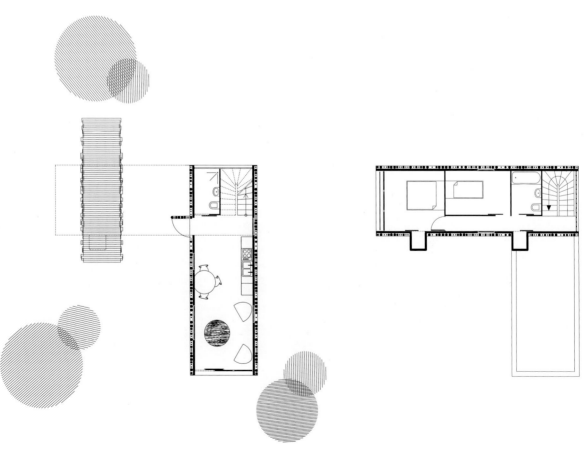

Floor plans

Modular Dwellings

Mobile

Edgar Blazona/Modular
Dwellings
www.modulardwellings.com
© Glen Campbell, Julia Blazona

161 sq ft (15 sq m)
1 bedroom

In situ assembly, metal structure,
corrugated metal and fiberglass
walls, plywood floor panels

The advantage of this modular system
is its ease of assembly as the user can
assemble, dismantle and transport the
house at a very low cost; this flexibility
is owing to the materials used. The
house stands on 6 concrete bases,
elevated about 8 in (20 cm) above the
ground to avoid leaks.

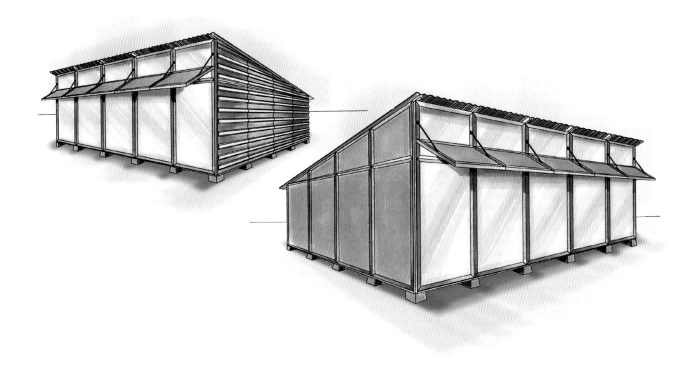

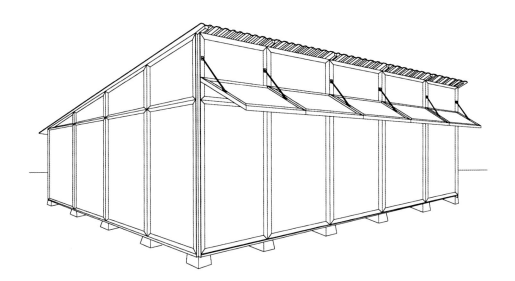

Axonometries

The simplicity of this design belies its best quality: its low-cost adaptability to any environment.

Portable House

Mobile

@

James&Mau
www.jamesandmau.com
© Antonio Corcuera

1,722 sq ft (160 sq m)
4 bedrooms, 3 washrooms

In situ assembly, steel shipping
containers, veneer modules,
cellulose and natural cork
insulation

This house can be adapted, expanded or
moved to meet the needs of a changing
world. This is a model made up of
spaces that can be added or removed
depending on the requirements; the
interior–exterior relationship can be
adjusted through the façade materials.

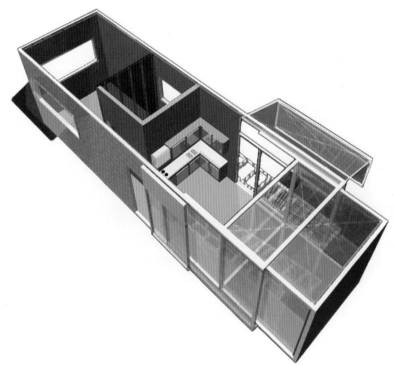

Axonometry

The house can be installed in different positions to take advantage of the best orientation depending on the regional climate.

Redondo Beach House

Redondo Beach, California, USA

DeMaria Design
www.demariadesign.com
© Andre Movsesyan, Christian
Kienapfel

3,229 sq ft (300 sq m)
3 bedrooms, 3 washrooms

In situ assembly, steel shipping
containers coated with pulverized
ceramic on the walls, wooden
structure, prefabricated joints

This house is made up of 40 ft (12 m) ISO
steel containers that arrive at the worksite
already fitted with the mechanical,
electrical and plumbing systems as well
as a timber frame and prefabricated
joints. The house is built in 180 days and
consumes 400 kW per container.

The roof has been clad in prefabricated metal panels and the sides covered with acrylic sheets.

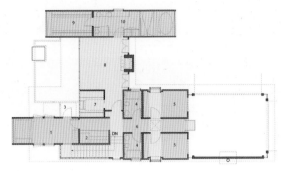

Second floor

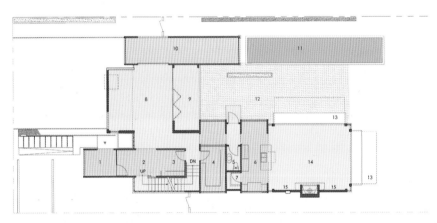

First floor

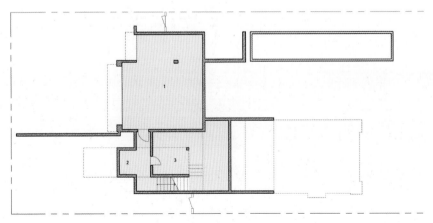

Basement floor

Garden Studio Mono

Mobile

Ecospace
www.ecospacestudios.com
© Ecospace

According to design

Factory assembled, SIPs, cedar
walls, green roof

Choosing between several
prefabricated models is an efficient
and environmentally friendly option
for a home. This house has certified
cedar walls, radiant floor heating, energy
efficient lighting, structural insulated
panels (SIPs) and it offers the option of
installing a green roof.

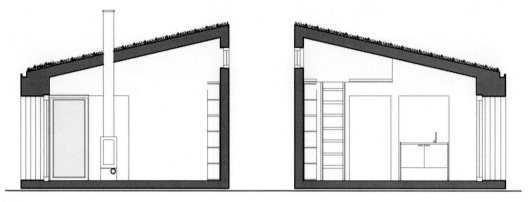

Sections

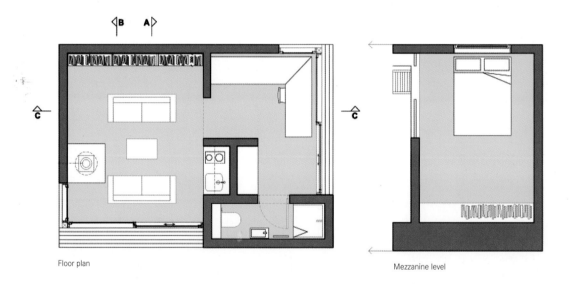

Floor plan

Mezzanine level

The roof panels are 9.4 in thick.
The radiant walls keep the home cool
in summer.

House of Steel and Wood

Ranón, Spain

Ecosistema Urbano
www.ecosistemaurbano.com
© Emilio P. Doiztua

969 sq ft (90 sq m)
1 bedroom, 2 washrooms

In situ assembly, steel and wood
structure, Douglas fir and local
pine paneling, glass expanses

The building is anchored to the ground
at only four points to respect the
environment and cause minimal impact
to the location. The structure is compact
and its central body is an irregular
prism-shape facing southeast to allow
the entry of as much natural light as
possible into the home.

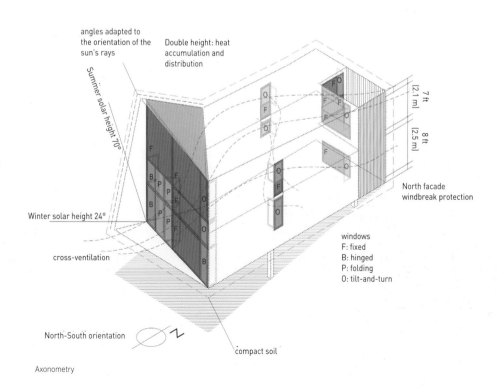

angles adapted to
the orientation of the
sun's rays

Double height: heat
accumulation and
distribution

Summer solar height 70°

7 ft
(2.1 m)

8 ft
(2.5 m)

North facade
windbreak protection

Winter solar height 24°

cross-ventilation

windows
F: fixed
B: hinged
P: folding
O: tilt-and-turn

North-South orientation

compact soil

Axonometry

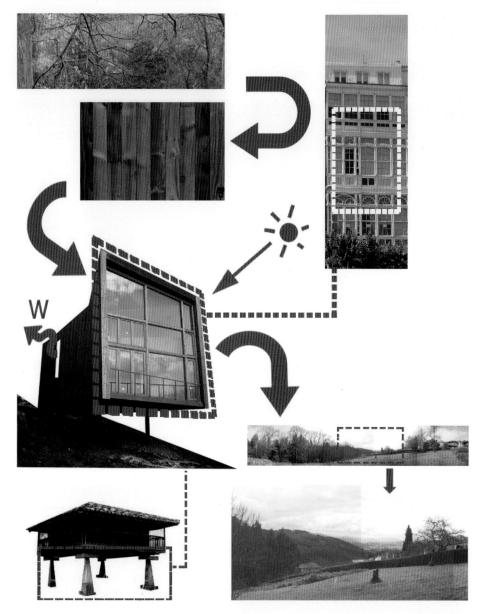

Diagram

The structure can be dismantled and recycled easily. The wooden interior prevents heat loss and promotes natural ventilation.

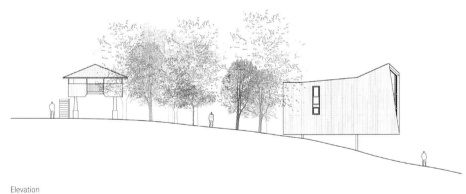

Elevation

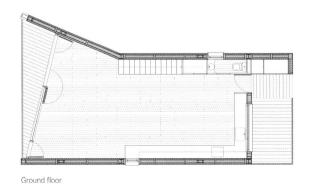

Ground floor

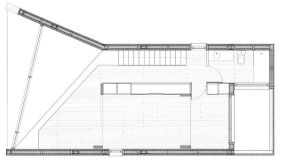

First floor

Floating Island

Mobile

Softroom Architects
www.softroom.com

700 sq ft (65 sq m)
1 bedroom

Factory pre-assembled modules,
in situ assembly, carbon fiber
module

This design is provisional, portable and
buoyant: a small shelter that can be
transported and anchored anywhere.
An artificial landscape is created in this
design: with a generator, the module
opens, the furniture inflates and a small
island unfurls.

This design is well suited to densely populated coastal cities, for which the product could be mass produced.

Nomadhome Trend Private 77c

Seekirchen am Wallersee, Austria

Hobby A. Schuster & Maul,
Gerold Peham
www.hobby-a.at
© Marc Haader

237 sq ft (22 sq m)
Basic module: 1 bedroom,
1 washroom

Factory assembled modules with
sandwich panel structure

Nomadhome is a patented flexible
construction system with modules
of 118 sq ft. Assembly takes 2 to
3 days. The use of sandwich panels
for the structure and system of
facilities, which are easily adaptable
between modules, allows you to
add an unlimited number of units.

The exterior façade can be covered with aluminum, copper, cast steel, black pine wood or PVC colored panels.

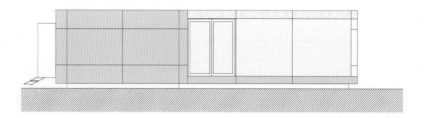

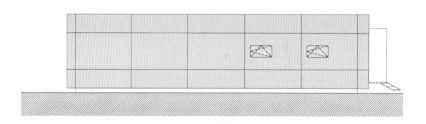

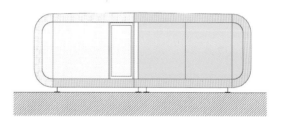

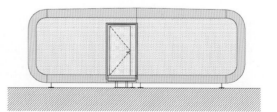

Elevations

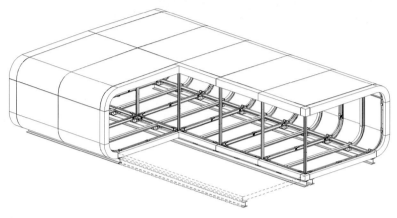

Axonometry

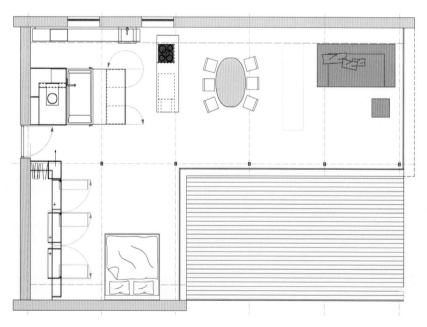

Floor plan

Stockner House

Tainach, Austria

Wolfgang Feyferlik
© Paul Ott

646 sq ft (60 sq m)
2 bedrooms, 1 washroom

In situ assembly, wood frame,
birch panels, zinc roof

The combination of materials — wood on
three façades, the glazed south side and
metal roof — creates a building with its
own language, which stands out but still
manages to respect its environment, a
combination of rustic and contemporary
style. The house is lifted off the ground
on wooden pilotis to emphasize the
weightlessness of the module.

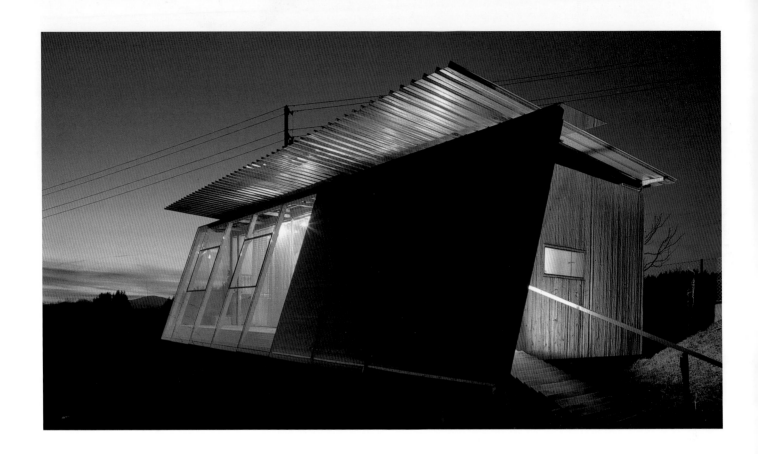

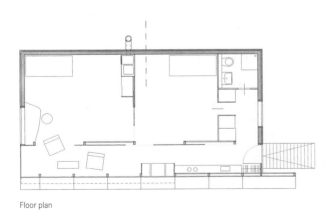

Floor plan

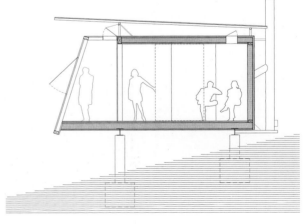

Section

Inside, a corridor connects two identical spaces that are delimited by mobile modules.

Study Box /
Read-Nest

Mobile

Dorte Mandrup Arkitekter
www.dortemandrup.dk
© Torben Eskerod,
Thomas Mandrup-Poulsen

105 sq ft (10 sq m)
1 bedroom

Factory assembled, timber frame
and natural wood slat walls

This small cabin is designed as an
additional space in the backyard for
reading, sleeping or simply relaxing.
Inside there are shelves and a foldable
bed if additional space is required.
A skylight positioned over the bed lets
you view the starry sky.

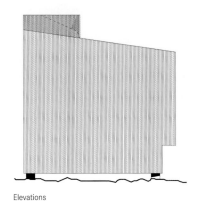  

Elevations

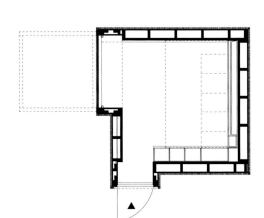 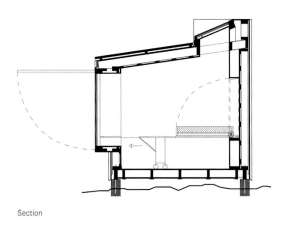

Floor plan

Section

This is a fully prefabricated
building that can be installed
on any type of land.

ONE WINDOW

ONE COVER

ONE NIGHT SKY

Diagrams

JOSHUA TREE

Mobile

Hangar Design Group
www.hangar.it
© Hangar Design Group

388 sq ft (36 sq m)
2 bedrooms, 2 washrooms

Factory assembled, coated steel
frame, zinc, titanium and wood,
larch wood planks and steel
sheets

This project was conceived as a
mountain retreat or vacation home,
inspired by Alpine shelters and their
gable roofs. The design facilitates
transport and adaptation to different
types of land on which the house can
be positioned. Moreover, this is a very
economical option.

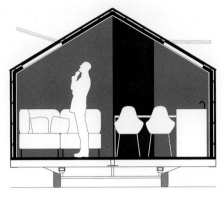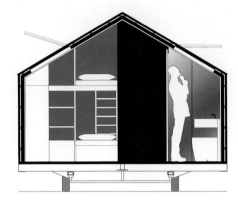

Sections

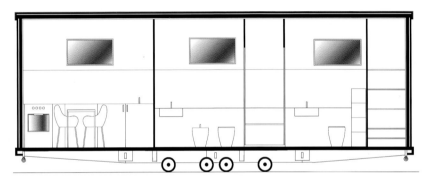

Longitudinal section

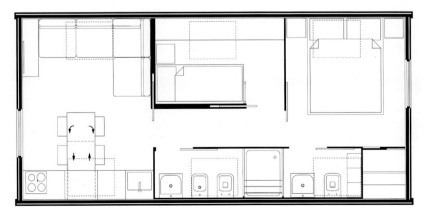

Floor plan

The internal structure allows you to rearrange the spaces according to the taste and needs of each user.

U + A HOUSE

Suitable for any location

Neil M. Denari Architects (NMDA)
www.denari.co
© Neil M. Denari Architects
(NMDA)

660–1,800 sq ft (61–167 sq m)
1 bedroom, 1 washroom

Factory assembled, three layer
panels: plywood, waterproof
membrane and aluminum

The architects devised a mini-tower that
mixed industrial concepts, contemporary
art and cutting-edge fashion. The
module is designed for three different
climates: hot and dry, warm and humid,
and continental and snow. It can be
installed in unusual places, and it is easy
to transport and install.

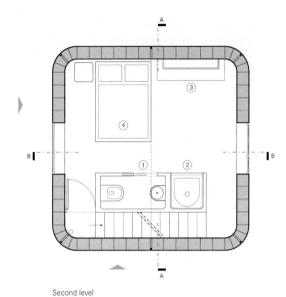

Second level

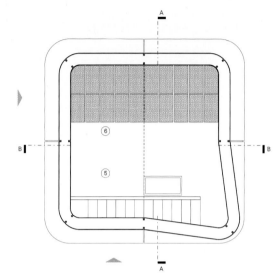

Roof plan

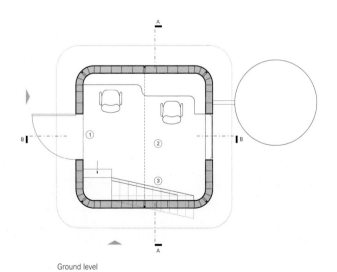

Ground level

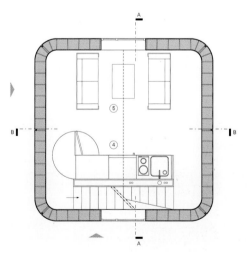

First level

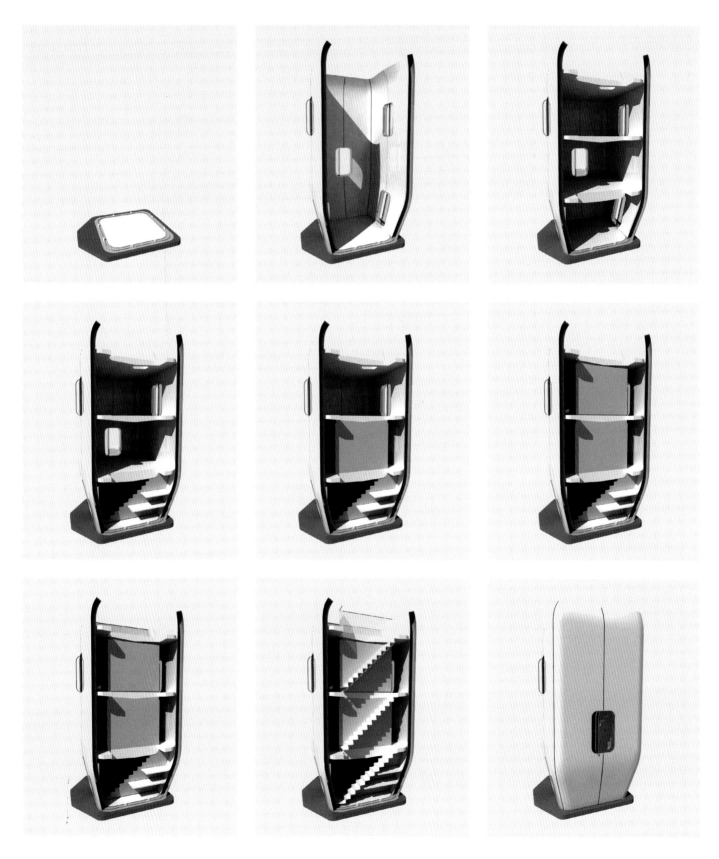

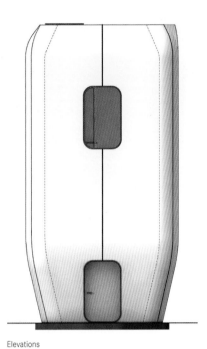

Elevations

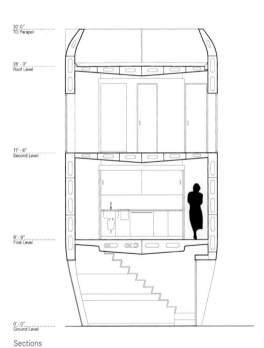
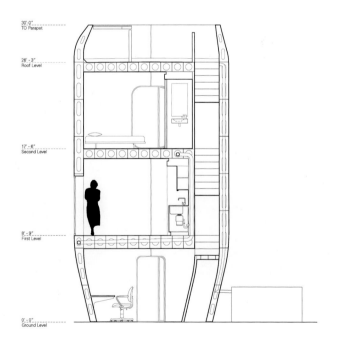

30'-0"
TO Parapet

26' - 3"
Roof Level

17' - 6"
Second Level

8' - 9"
First Level

0' - 0"
Ground Level

30'-0"
TO Parapet

26' - 3"
Roof Level

17' - 6"
Second Level

8' - 9"
First Level

0' - 0"
Ground Level

Sections

The basic module is made up of eight panels that form an area of 16 x 16 ft (5 x 5 m) and 30 ft (9 m) high.

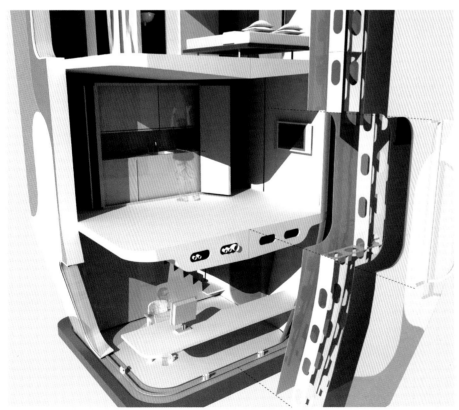

HIGASHI-OSAKA HOUSE

Osaka, Japan

Waro Kishi
www.k-associates.com
© Tomiko Hirai

1,991 sq ft (185 sq m)
2 bedrooms, 2 washrooms

In situ assembly, steel structure,
prefabricated concrete panels,
steel

The architect created an innovative
interior layout from a sequence of
courtyards that are connected to the
rooms of the house, and that lead the
way inside the house and onto the
terraces. The steel frame is covered with
prefabricated concrete panels and large
glass expanses.

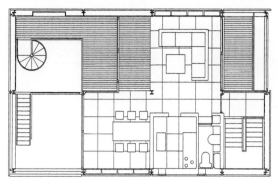

Second floor

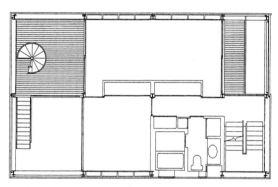

First floor

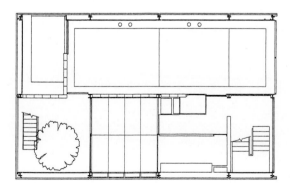

Ground floor

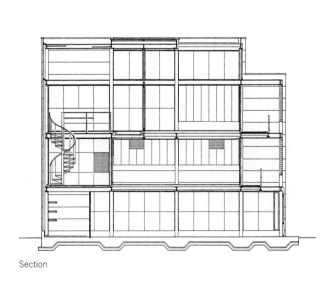

Section

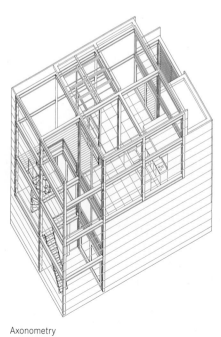

Axonometry

Large openings, glass and white planes emphasize the connections between the interior and exterior.

CAMP WILDALPEN

Wildalpen, Austria

Holz Box
www.holzbox.at
© Birgit Koell

2,637 sq ft (245 sq m)
2 bedrooms, 1 washroom

In situ assembly, pine structure
and enclosure

The building, elevated off the ground,
consists of five modules for the homes
and one for the communal area.
Each module has an area measuring
376 sq ft (35 sq m), and each home
has a central core which houses the
bathrooms and kitchens. Some pieces
of furniture, such as the bunk beds,
are built-in.

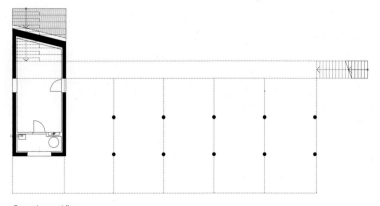

General ground floor

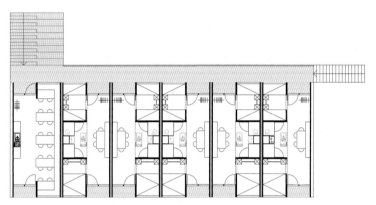

General first floor

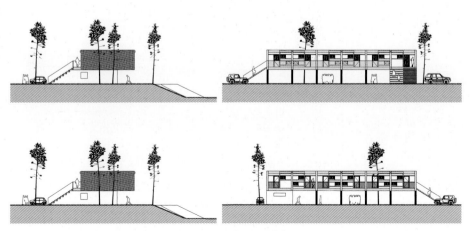

Elevations

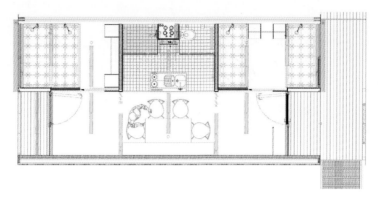

Floor plan

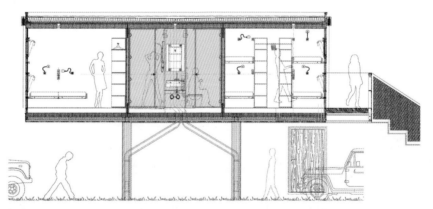

Section

The layout of the internal spaces allows the bedrooms to enjoy ample natural light.

ITHOUSE

Pioneertown, California, USA

Taalman Koch Architecture
www.taalmankoch.com
© Art Gray

1,100 sq ft (102 sq m)

Factory pre-assembled modules,
in situ assembly, aluminum frame,
steel roof, glass walls, solar panels

This home consists of a package
that includes the structural system,
the inner closets and the enclosure.
The components of the house are
transported in parts and assembly
instructions are included. It only takes
two people to erect the building and
the assembly process is rapid.

The design calls for patterns to be placed on the glass panels to frame views; they create shade from the sun and incorporate the house into the desert landscape.

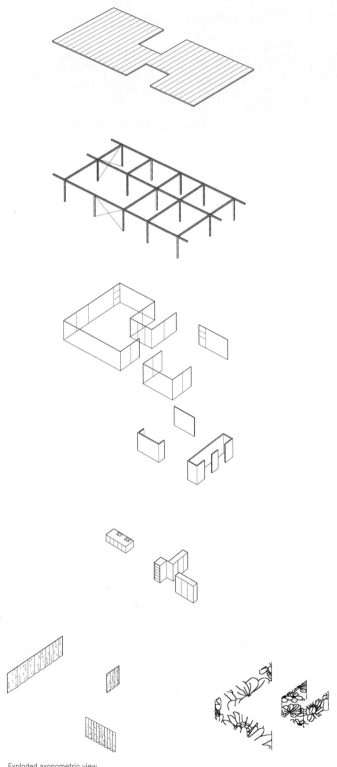

Exploded axonometric view

BURST* 003

North Haven, Australia

System Architects
www.systemarchitects.net
© Floto + Warner

1,001 sq ft (93 sq m)
3 bedrooms, 2 washrooms

In situ assembly, wood frame,
plywood panels, steel and glass

Natural light is the main design concept:
in the dining room, the light is reflected
in two directions while the lounge is
located at a central point. Temperature
comfort is guaranteed by passive
systems. The home is erected on stilts
6.5 ft (2 m) high, allowing the cool air
from beneath to circulate.

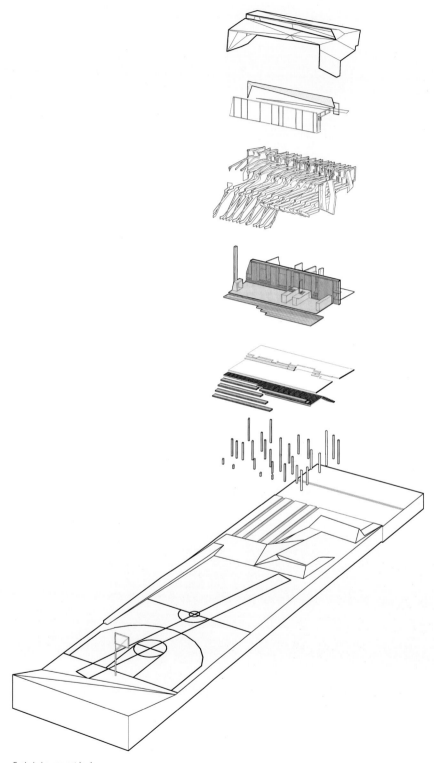

Exploded axonometric view

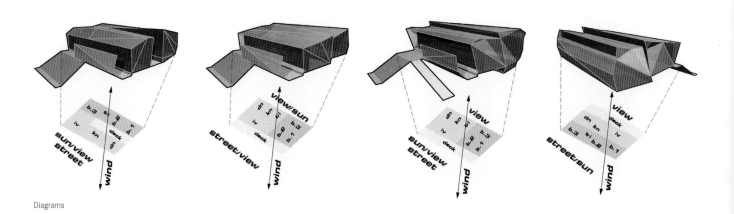

Diagrams

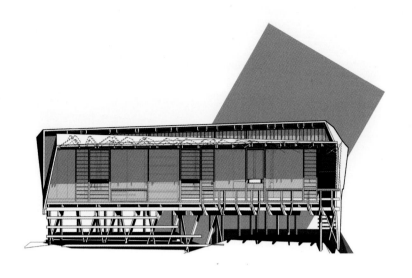

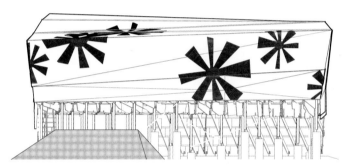

Elevations

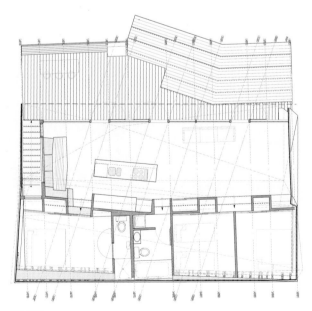

Floor plan

This design is a real alternative
to mass production models, as it has
emerged from geometric variations.

TREE HOUSE

Mobile

Softroom Architects
www.softroom.com

1 bedroom

In situ assembly, steel, plastic
and elastic

This small module was designed for the
magazine *Wallpaper*; the goal was to
join a construction to a tree trunk while
causing minimal impact. The structure,
a set of rings that supports a triangular
frame, is designed to support the
various components of the home.

A dining table, plumbing facilities and a foldable bed can be adjoined to the structure.

BARK STUDIO

Noosa Hinterland, Australia

Bark Design Pty Ltd
www.barkdesign.com.au
© Christopher Frederick Jones,
Vincent Long

1,076 sq ft (100 sq m)
1 bedroom, 2 washrooms

In situ assembly, steel structure,
plywood sheets, glass panels

This building was erected in just six days,
with a 66 ft (20 m) long rectangular
modular structure of plywood modules
forming the floors, ceilings and walls. The
finishes are carried out using fixed and
movable glass in three of the façades
and plywood panels in the fourth.

The design is aimed to respect the environment, maximize cross-ventilation, use lightweight materials and be resistant to earthquakes.

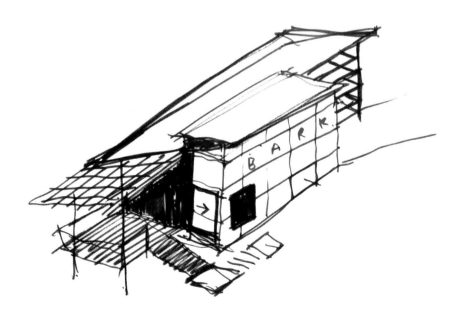

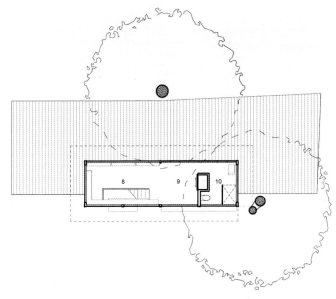

Mezzanzine level

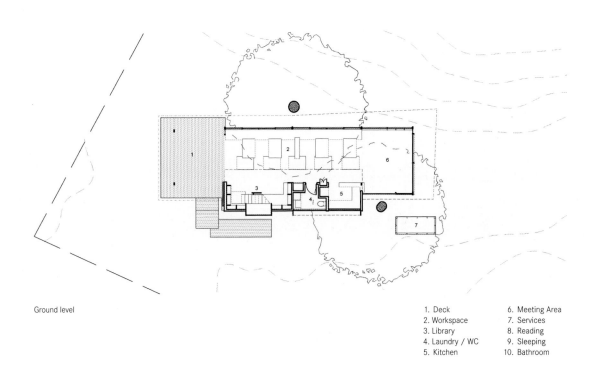

Ground level

1. Deck
2. Workspace
3. Library
4. Laundry / WC
5. Kitchen
6. Meeting Area
7. Services
8. Reading
9. Sleeping
10. Bathroom

SUNSET CABIN

Lake Simcoe, Canada

Taylor Smyth Architects
www.taylorsmyth.com
© Peter Gumpesberger,
Toni Hafkenscheid

323 sq ft (30 sq m)
1 bedroom, 1 washroom

In situ assembly, plywood and
cedar structure and walls

This cabin was built in a month
in a square in Toronto. It was then
dismantled and sorted into pieces and
reassembled by the lake in just 10 days.
The prefabricated construction is lifted
off the ground on two reinforced steel
beams over four concrete pilotis.

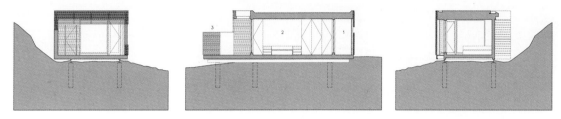

Sections

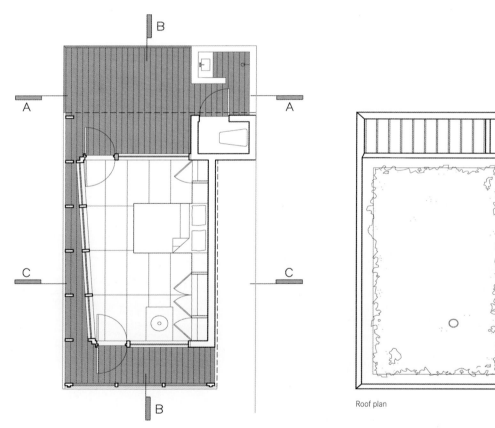

B

A ———— A

C ———— C

B

Ground floor

Roof plan

The shutters provide protection from the heat and create a second layer of insulation, which is useful in both summer and winter.

ANNIE RESIDENCE

Austin, Texas, USA

Bercy Chen Studio
www.bcarc.com
© Mike Osborne, Joseph
Pettyjohn

2,000 sq ft (186 sq m)
2 bedrooms, 1 washroom

In situ assembly, steel modular
frame with thermo-insulating
panels, concrete floors

Two pavilions connected by a glass
corridor make up the structure of the
house. Each volume has a central core
with a steel structure covered with red
or blue acrylic panels. The bedrooms
are arranged around a central courtyard,
and the interior partitions can be
opened to create cross ventilation.

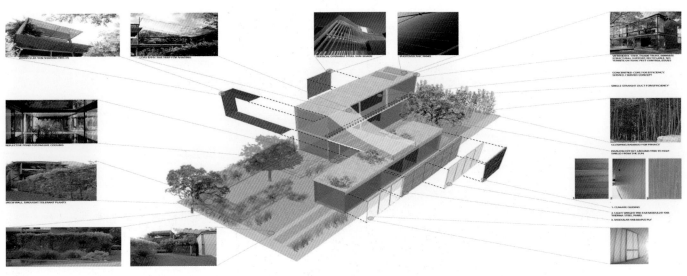

Diagram

This design is influenced by Moorish Asian and Japanese architecture.

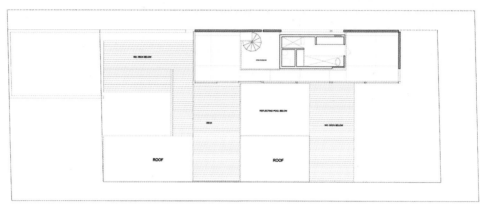

First floor

Ground floor

REF-RING

Zushi, Japan

Yasuhiro Yamashita/
Atelier Tekuto
www.tekuto.com
© Makoto Yoshida

700 sq ft (65 sq m)
3 bedrooms, 1 washroom

In situ assembly, prestressed
wood panels

The architects created a home in
which space is affected by a sense
of ambiguity. The arrangement of
the panels at odd angles creates
three-dimensional areas that make
the house look distorted. Each wooden
panel is prestressed with a steel cable
running through it.

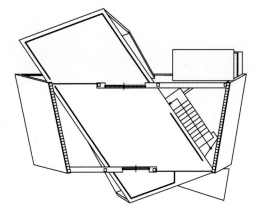

First floor

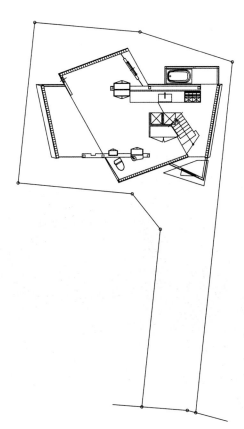

Ground floor

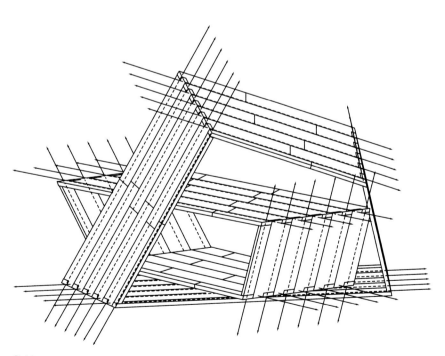

Sketch

Sections

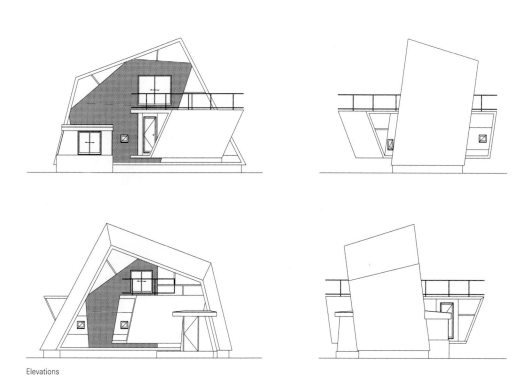

Elevations

The house is formed by the intersection of two irregular structures. Inside, the layout presents an innovative use of space.

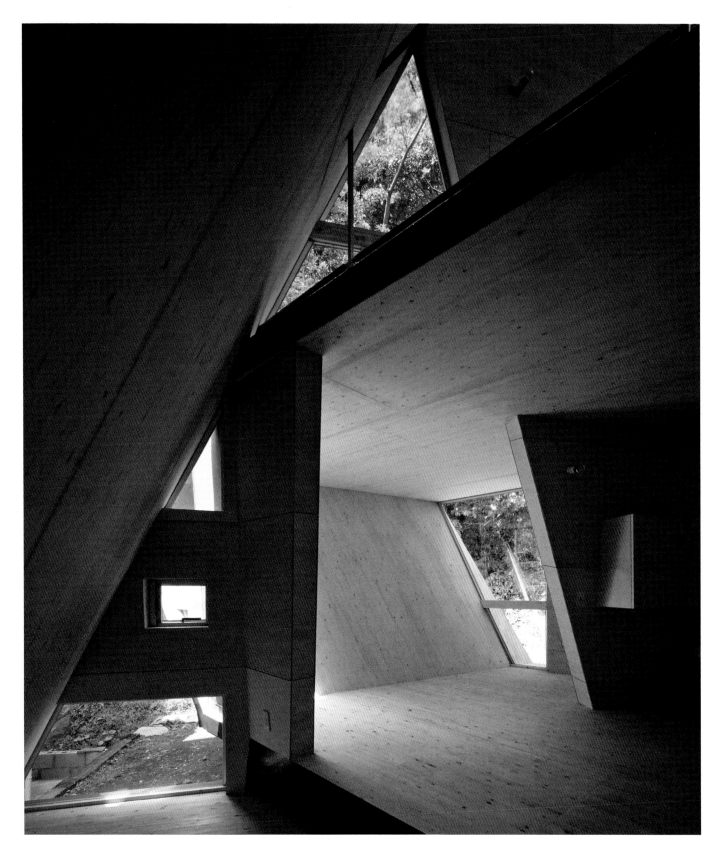

SOLAR ACTIVE HOUSE

Kraig, Austria

Architekturbüro Reinberg
www.reinberg.net
© Sonnenkraft Österreich,
Horst Danner

1,615 sq ft (150 sq m)

In situ assembly, wooden
structure, prefabricated pine wood
panels, photovoltaic modules

This house is self-sufficient as it
produces all the energy it consumes.
The triple pane insulation and heat
recovery systems reduce temperature
loss. The windows open automatically
when there is a lack of oxygen or excess
moisture in the interior.

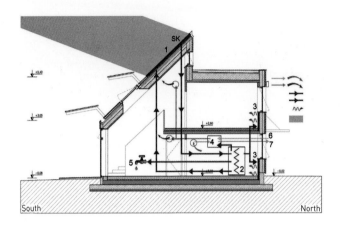

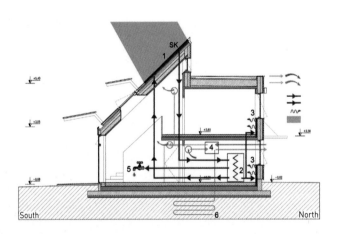

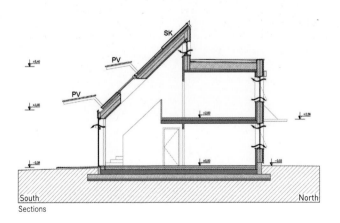

Sections

The home's components include a domestic hot water tank and 264 sq ft (24 sq m) of solar thermal collectors on the roof.

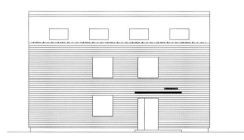

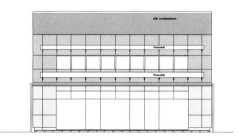

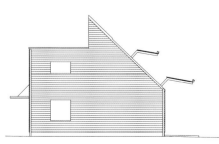

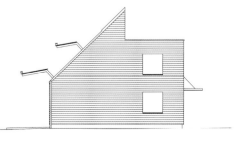

Elevations

GABLE HOUSE

Urbana-Champaign, Illinois, USA

University of Illinois
www.solardecathlon.illinois.edu
© University of Illinois

807 sq ft (75 sq m)
1 bedroom, 1 washroom

In situ assembly, bamboo
structure, recycled wood walls,
solar panels

The primary concept of the Gable
House is to form a synthesis between
innovative technology and vernacular
Midwestern American architecture,
creating an environmentally sustainable
home designed to be transported
prebuilt to its final location.

198

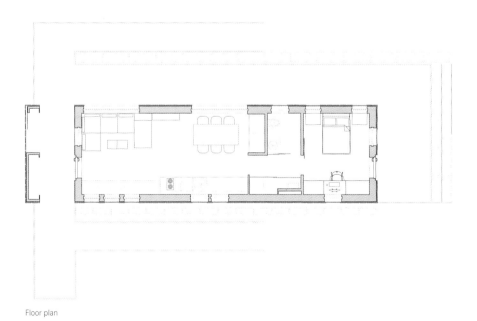

Floor plan

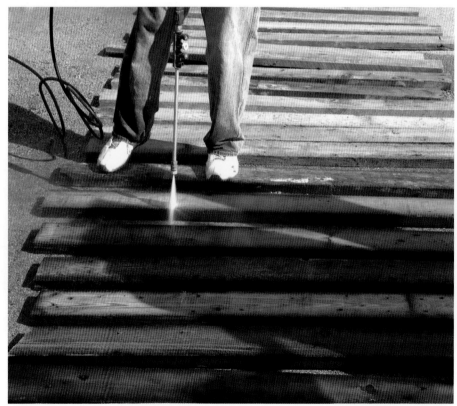

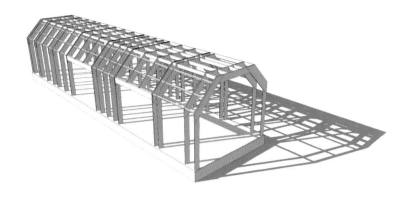

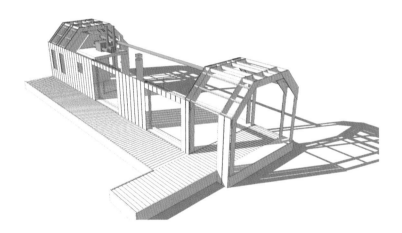

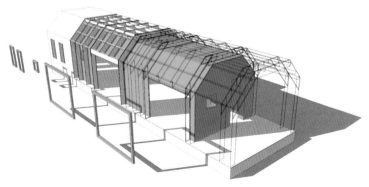

Axonometries

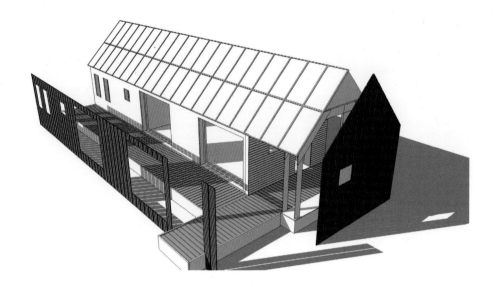

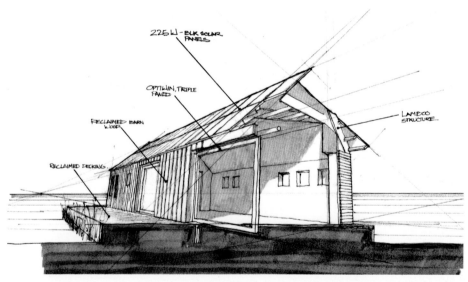

225W - BLK SOLAR PANELS

OPTIWIN, TRIPLE PANED

LAMBOO STRUCTURE

RECLAIMED BARN WOOD

RECLAIMED DECKING

Axonometry and sketch

Despite the size, the interior is spacious and comfortable. The layout can be changed to include more rooms.

KOSOVO KIT

Mobile

System Architects
www.systemarchitects.net

1,076 sq ft (100 sq m)
1 bedroom

Factory pre-assembled modules,
in situ assembly, corrugated
machine cut metal panels,
polycarbonate panels for windows

This kit creates a shelter that can be
transported anywhere; it is easily built
and maintained with limited resources.
It consists of corrugated metal sandwich
panels with a polystyrene center,
forming a resilient, self-supporting
structure.

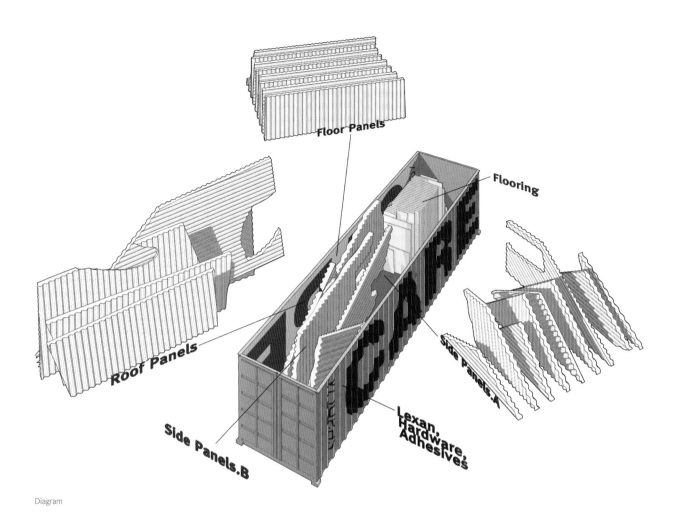

Diagram

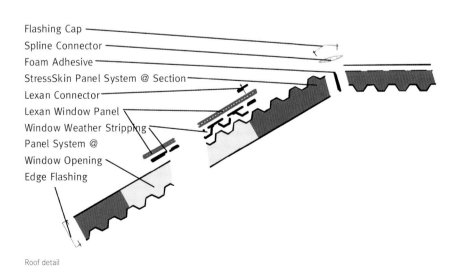

Flashing Cap
Spline Connector
Foam Adhesive
StressSkin Panel System @ Section
Lexan Connector
Lexan Window Panel
Window Weather Stripping
Panel System @
Window Opening
Edge Flashing

Roof detail

Each box contains the components
necessary to build one shelter,
which typically takes about a day
to complete.

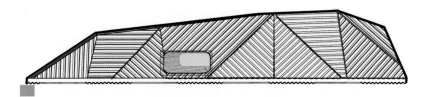

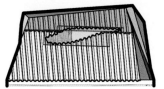

Elevations

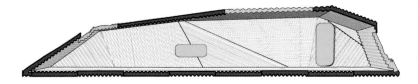

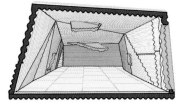

Sections

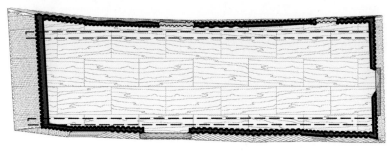

Floor plan

PALLET HOUSE

Mobile

I-Beam Design
www.i-beamdesign.com
© I-Beam Design

270 sq ft (25 sq m)
1 bedroom

In situ assembly, wooden pallets

This project was conceived as a form of low-cost, easily constructed housing for refugees. It is a versatile, sustainable and recyclable option built with wooden pallets. A basic shelter made from 100 pallets adapts to any climate and the needs of users, and can be built in less than one week.

The use of recycled materials facilitates the dismantling and deconstruction once they reach the end of their useful life.

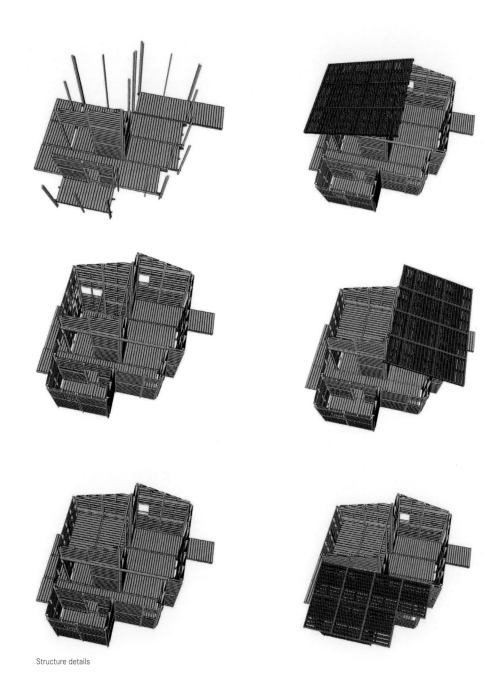

Structure details

TALIESIN MOD.FAB

Scottsdale, Arizona, USA

Office of Mobile Design by
Jennifer Siegal, Michael P.
Johnson Design Studio, Taliesin /
Frank Lloyd Wright School
of Architecture
www.designmobile.com
© Bill Timmerman

960 sq ft (89 sq m)
1 bedroom, 1 washroom

In situ assembly, SIPs

This is a simple and sustainable
home suitable for arid regions. The
typical layout consists of a bedroom,
washroom, kitchen, living room and
covered terrace, however, the spaces
can be reconfigured. The building was
designed so that it could be connected
to the power grid or remain off-grid.

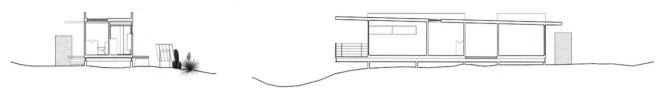

Sections

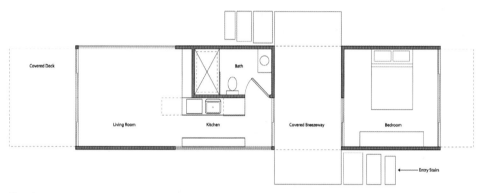

Covered Deck

Bath

Living Room   Kitchen   Covered Breezeway   Bedroom

Entry Stairs

Floor plan

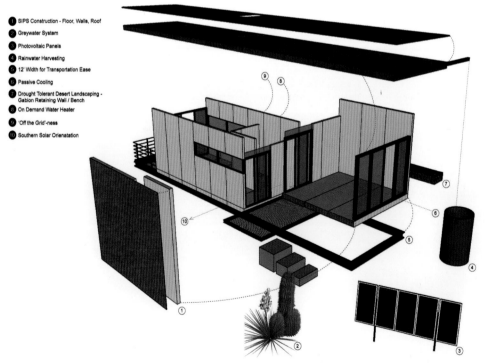

1 SIPS Construction - Floor, Walls, Roof
2 Greywater System
3 Photovoltaic Panels
4 Rainwater Harvesting
5 12' Width for Transportation Ease
6 Passive Cooling
7 Drought Tolerant Desert Landscaping - Gabion Retaining Wall / Bench
8 On Demand Water Heater
9 'Off the Grid'-ness
10 Southern Solar Orienatation

Exploded axonometric view

The structure is sized and designed to be transported by truck, reduce costs and speed up the construction process.

SOMMERHUS
I JØRLUNDE

Jørlunde, Denmark

Dorte Mandrup Arkitekter
www.dortemandrup.dk
© Torben Eskerod

2,153 sq ft (200 sq m)
3 bedrooms, 2 washrooms

In situ assembly, prefabricated
wall panels

Built at ground level, the interior terraces
are connected to the outside through
prefabricated movable partitions. The
courtyards are arranged to allow the
entry of light and heat in every room
of the house.

Sliding panels form new areas to cool down the space and light up corners.

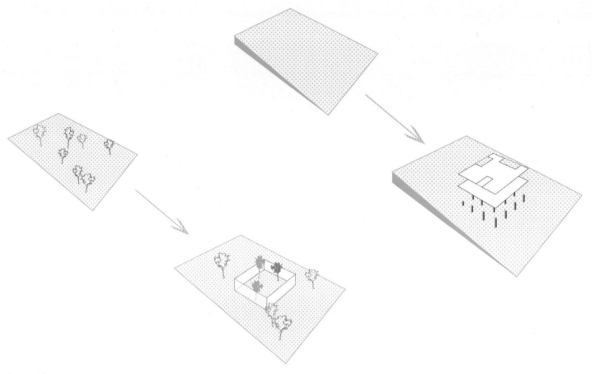

Axonometries

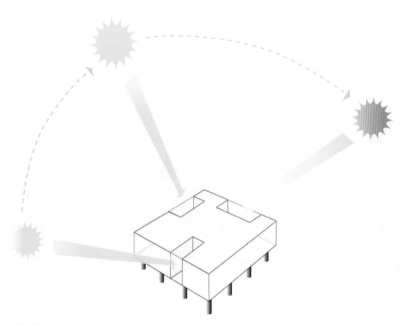

Solar diagram

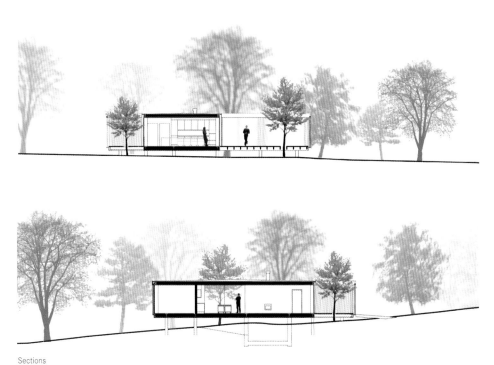

Sections

Floor plan

The floor plan labels, reading from top:

- study
- study
- kitchen/dining
- terrace (west)
- terrace (east)
- bathroom
- living
- bathroom
- sauna
- entrance
- winter-garden
- access terrace (south)
- bridge

BB

BERKSHIRE HOUSE

West Stockbridge,
Massachusetts, USA

Resolution: 4 Architecture
www.re4a.com
© Resolution: 4 Architecture

2,227 sq ft (207 sq m)
2 bedrooms, 2 washrooms

Factory pre-assembled modules,
in situ assembly, cedar paneling,
bamboo floors

The prefabricated parts of this house
were built in the factory and assembled
onsite to reduce the environmental
impact. This home uses geothermal
energy for heating and air conditioning.
On the top floor, two terraces connect
users directly to the exterior.

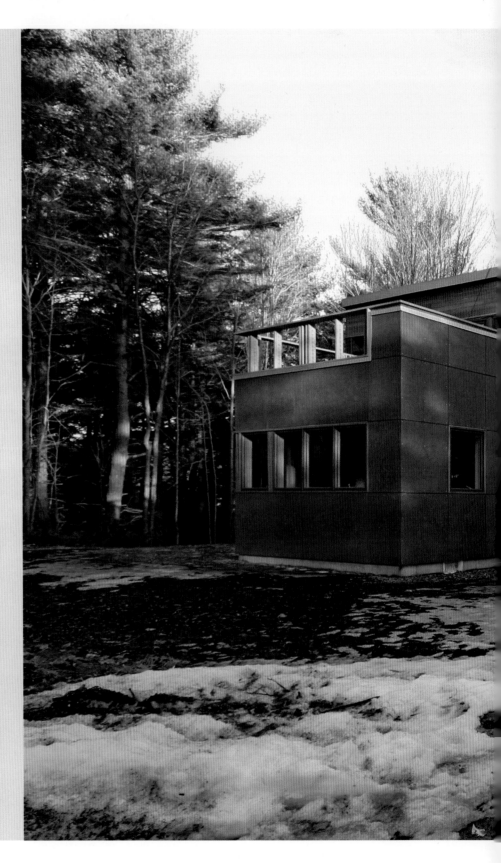

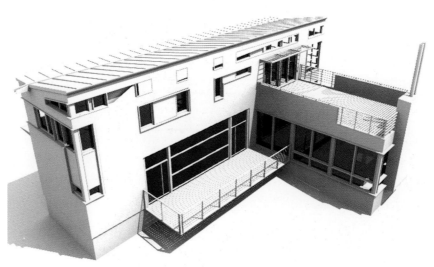

Axonometries

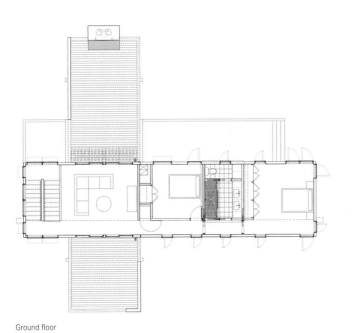
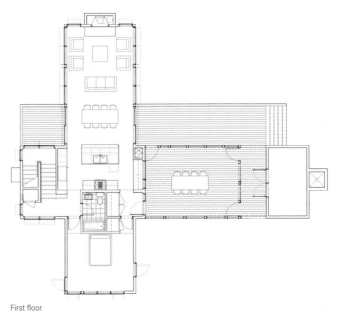

Ground floor   First floor

The covered gallery on the lower floor creates a unique space during the warmer months.

WOODEN MODULES

London, United Kingdom

Arthur Collin/DAAM
www.daam.co.uk

1-2 bedrooms, 1 washroom

In situ assembly, wooden
structure and panels

This design promotes high density areas
and ensures the use and maintenance
of public areas; buildings of different
heights are merged to create a diverse
urban environment. Each house consists
of a solid wood frame and the main
walls incorporate the key elements.

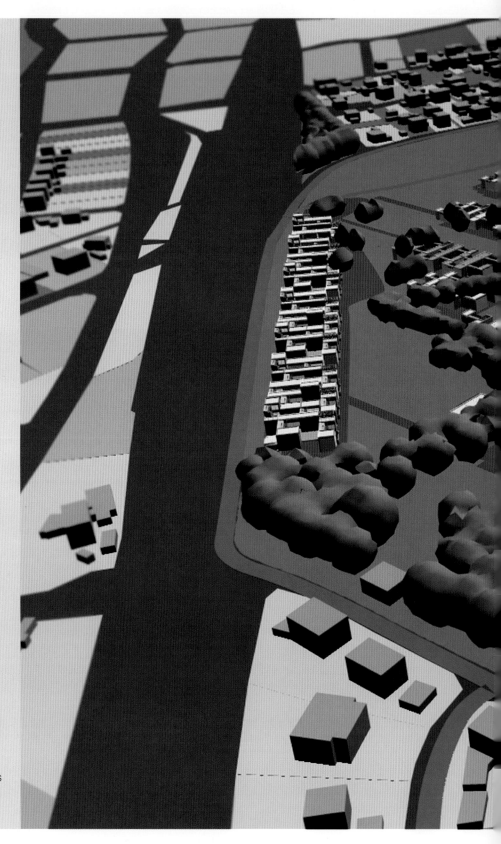

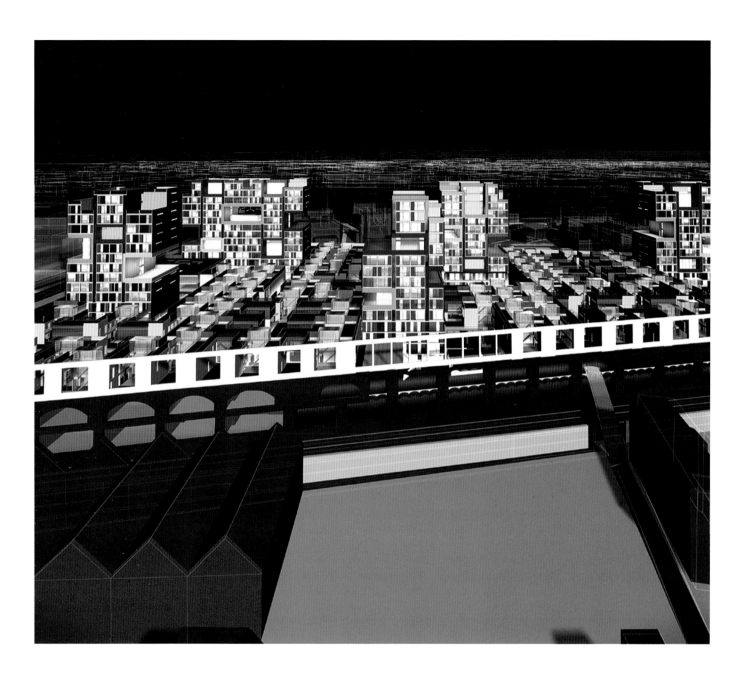

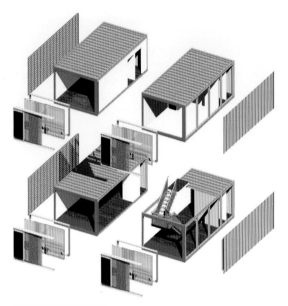
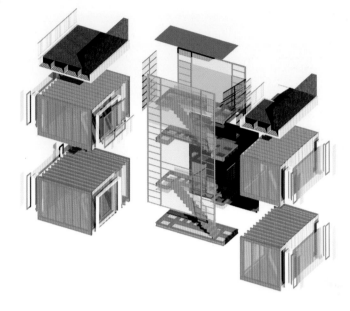

Exploded axonometric views

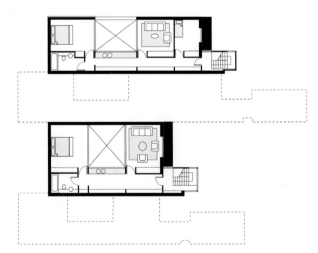
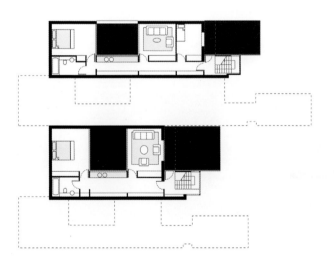

Single house possibilities

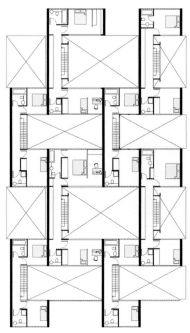
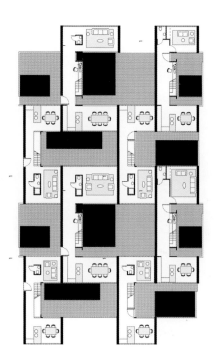

Multi-family building possibilities

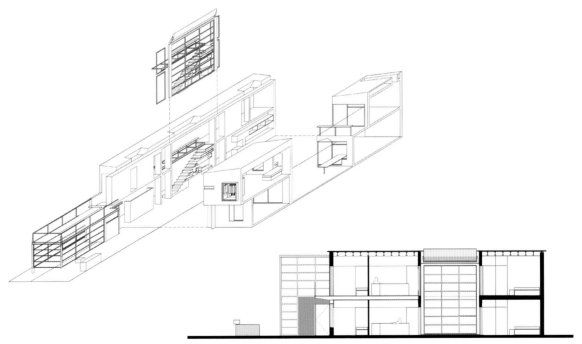

Axonometric section and section

Interior spaces are adaptable to the needs of the inhabitants, who may add or remove modules.

HOUSE OF FURNITURE PARTS

Milan, Italy

Studio Makkink & Bey
www.studiomakkinkbey.nl
© Nicoló Degiorgis, Droog

Area according to design,
1 bedroom

In situ assembly, plywood panels

This house plays with the concept of the contained and the container. This pavilion can be built within an existing space and contains a storage system for furniture in its walls. The pieces are cut and numbered for easy assembly and subsequent storage.

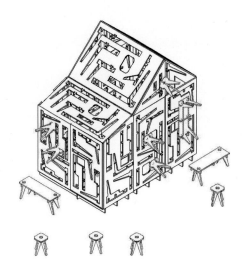

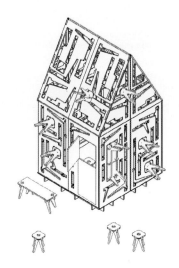

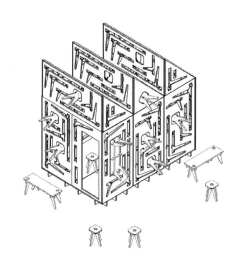

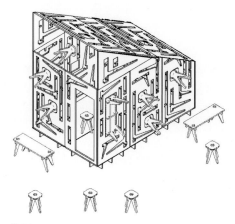

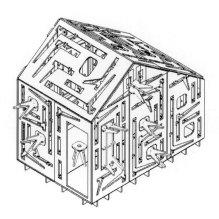

Sketches

The materials can be produced locally, the stacked panels are easily transported and each design is adapted to the different functions.

PECONIC BAY HOUSE

Shinnecock Hills, New York, USA

Resolution: 4 Architecture
www.re4a.com
© Resolution: 4 Architecture

2,004 sq ft (186 sq m)
3 bedrooms, 2 washrooms

Factory pre-assembled modules,
in situ assembly, cedar wood and
cement walls, photovoltaic panels

This project is considered sustainable
due to several of its features: its
prefabricated parts are produced
under a strict waste management
program, its time-saving construction
methods reduce environmental impact,
and the plants that accompany the
house were chosen for their level of
drought resistance.

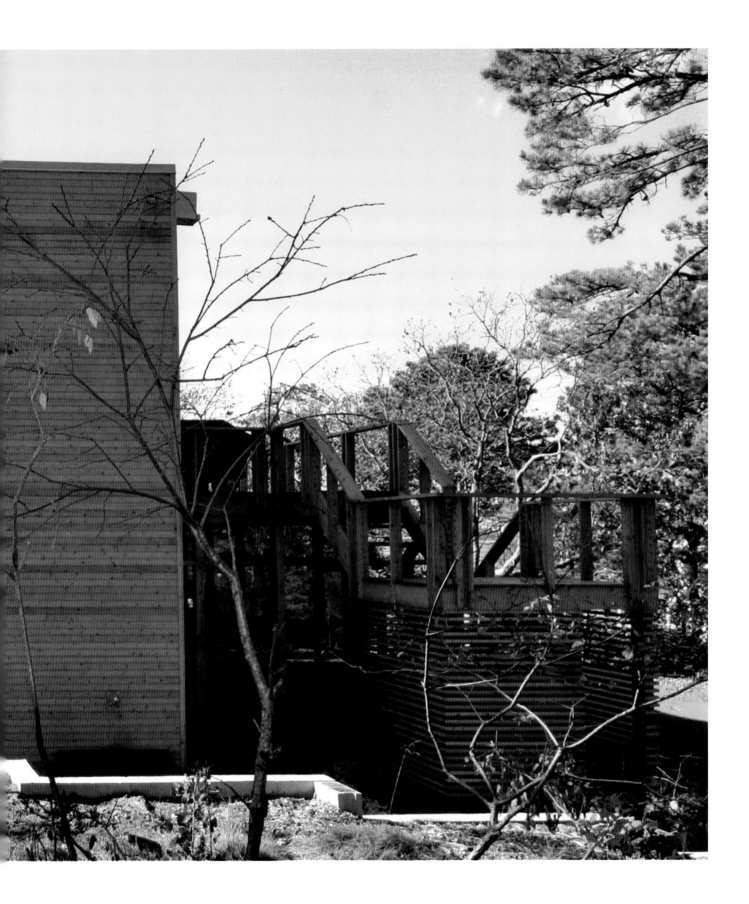

Axonometry

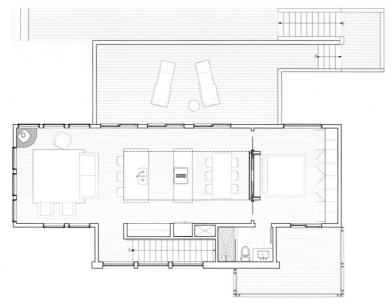

First floor

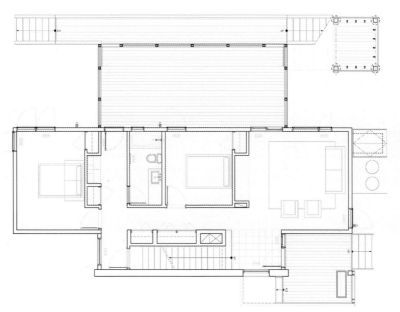

Ground floor

The electricity comes exclusively from photovoltaic panels and geothermal energy.

272

RINCON

Mobile

Marmol Radziner Prefab
www.marmolradzinerprefab.com
© Tyler Boye

660 sq ft (61 sq m)
1 bedroom, 1 washroom

Factory pre-assembled modules,
in situ assembly, SIPs, bamboo
flooring, non-toxic paints

This company's models are factory
assembled and transported to the site.
There is the option of including these
sustainable features: solar panels,
insulation from recycled materials,
recycled steel frame, LED lighting, or
UV protection windows.

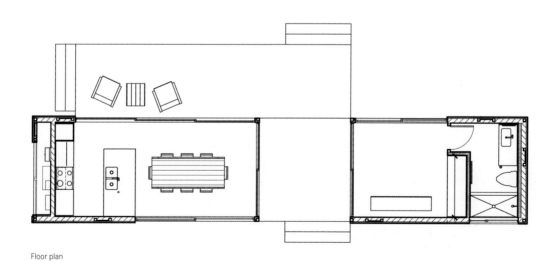

Floor plan

SIPs reduce the need for electricity for heating and air conditioning by about 12 to 14 percent.

ESSEX STREET HOUSE

Brunswick, Australia

Andrew Maynard Architects
www.maynardarchitects.com
© Peter Bennetts, Dan Mahon

1 bedroom, 2 washrooms

In situ assembly, iron structure,
GRC type stud-frame panels,
red cedar strips

The aim of this project was to extend a
typical suburban home while improving
its eco-friendliness; notable features
include sun screens constructed of
recycled wood, improved insulation, a
gray-water tank and a space for a future
solar panel installation.

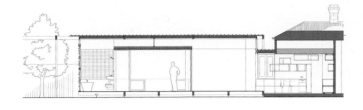

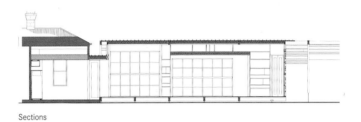

Sections

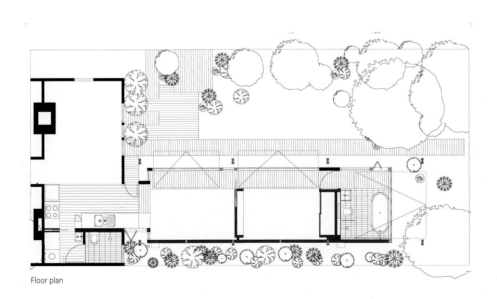

Floor plan

Affixed to one façade is a tank to collect rainwater, and the roof has been designed to incorporate solar panels.

PEN HOUSE

Mauerbach, Austria

Querkraft Architects
www.querkraft.at
© Hertha Harnaus

1,023 sq ft (95 sq m)
2 bedrooms, 3 washrooms

Factory pre-assembled parts,
in situ assembly, wood panels
and frames

This project consists of one large box-
like structure, assembled in a day. Little
adaptation is required of the structure,
wood panels and other woodwork once
out of the factory. Inside, rigid walls were
avoided and flexible and open spaces
were chosen. The staircase divides the
daytime and nighttime areas.

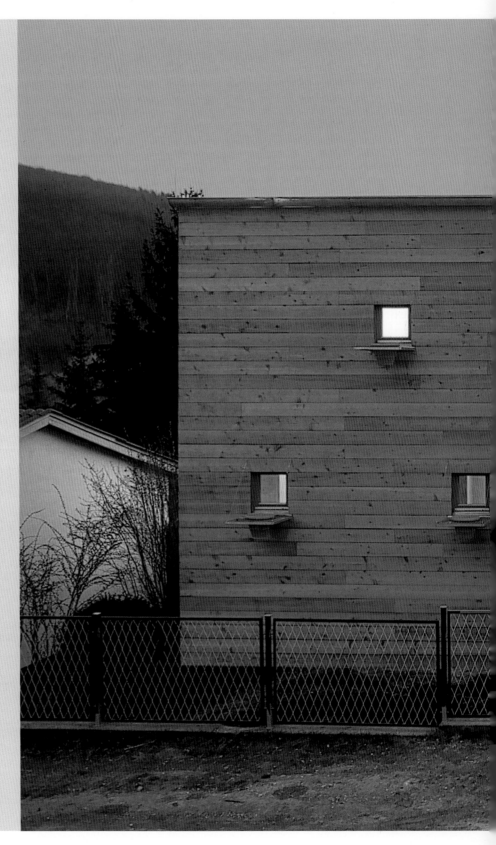

Betreten der
Baustelle
verboten!
Eltern haften für ihre Kinder!

querkraft

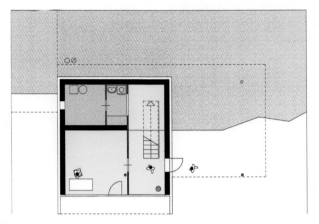

Second floor

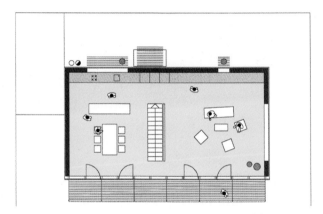

First floor

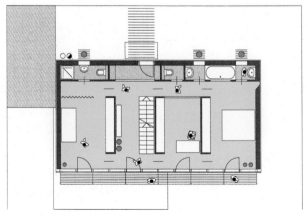

Ground floor

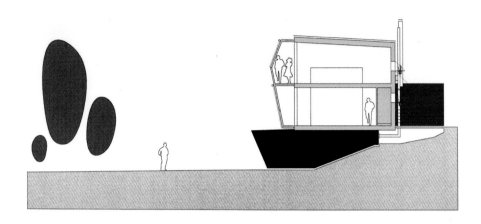

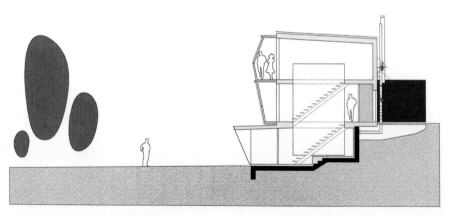

Sections

The size of the balconies varies depending on the requirements for each floor: the living space level is allocated a large balcony for lounging, whereas the bedroom level's balcony is smaller.

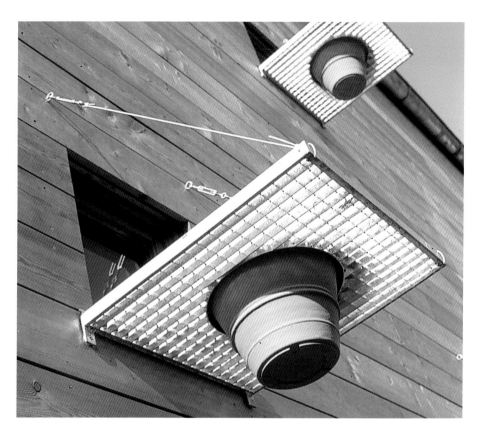

MTGH

Suitable for any location

Philippe Barriere Collective
www.philippebarrierecollective.com
© Philippe Barriere Collective

390–540 sq ft (36–50 sq m)
1-2 bedrooms, 1 washroom

In situ assembly, structure,
aluminum roof and interior walls,
glass and Galvalume enclosure,
concrete floors

Modular Transitional Growth Housing
(MTGH) modules can be combined
to form structures of innumerable
uses (such as offices, retail spaces
and homes) of up to three stories.
Recyclable materials and materials
resilient to climate change are used.
The façades are transparent and the
roofs are vaulted.

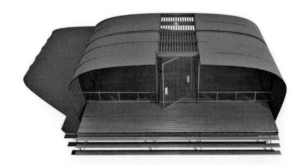

Axonometries

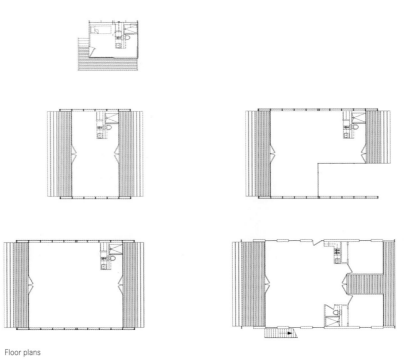

Floor plans

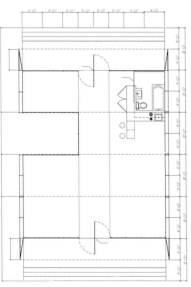

Option 1

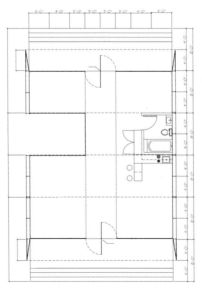

Option 2

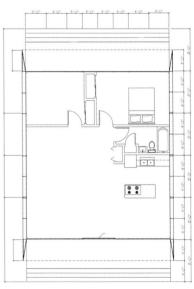

Option 3

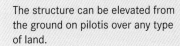

The structure can be elevated from the ground on pilotis over any type of land.

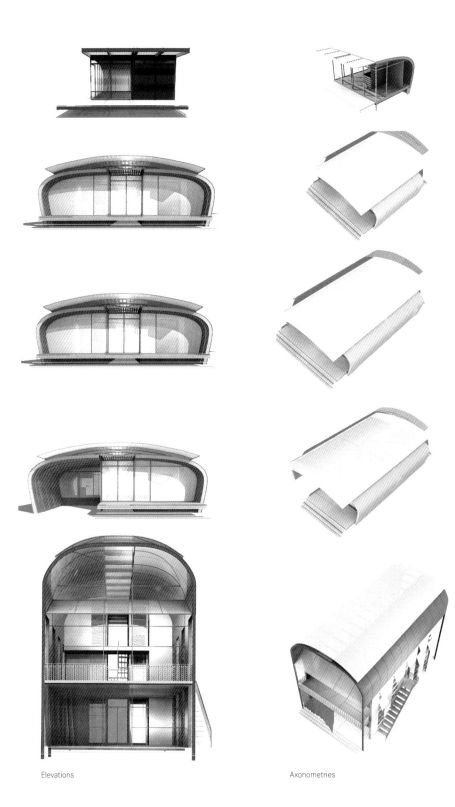

Elevations   Axonometries

THE QUICK HOUSE

Tewksbury, New Jersey, USA

Adam Kalkin/Quik Build
www.quik-build.com
© Peter Aaron/ESTO

2,004 sq ft (186 sq m)
3 bedrooms, 3 washrooms

Factory pre-assembled modules,
in situ assembly, steel shipping
containers, glass panels

This industrial-style house is built from
shipping containers. The modules are
completed in the factory; once on-site,
after the electrical, plumbing and glass
panels are installed, the home is sprayed
with a waterproof membrane and finally
a green roof is installed.

Construction and assembly time is 3 months. This house has 2 volumes with additional functions.

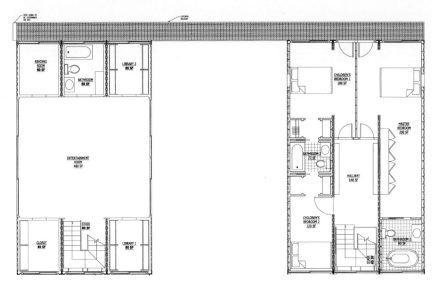

First floor

Ground floor

FLAKE HOUSE

Nantes, France

Olgga Architectes
www.olgga.fr
© Fabienne Delafraye

237 sq ft (22 sq m)
1 bedroom, 1 washroom

In situ assembly, wooden
structure and walls

This modular wooden refuge, inspired
by the tradition of the *Folies de bois*, is
supported by a structure built entirely
in the factory and divided for easy
transport. This module offers two rooms
that can be combined into a straight
line, a T-shape or an L-shape.

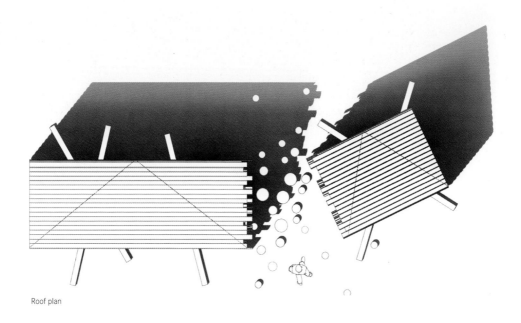

Roof plan

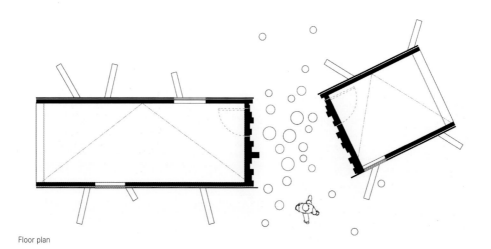

Floor plan

The structure is separated to
establish a spatial borderline and
therefore enhance the access to
the house.

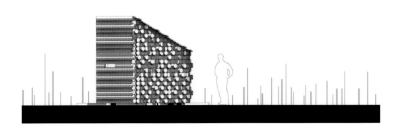

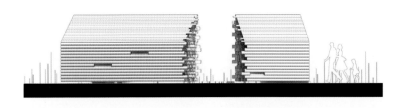

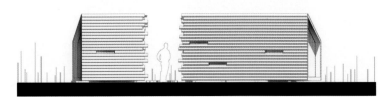

Elevations

MARTIN RESIDENCE ADDITION

Berkeley, California, USA

Jason Langkammerer,
John Barone/@6 Architecture
www.at-six.com
© Adrian Gregorutti

845 sq ft (79 sq m)
1 bedroom, 1 washroom

In situ assembly and factory
trimmed cement façade panels,
bamboo closets and flooring,
polycarbonate and glass walls,
photovoltaic panels

This two story volume is an extension of
the original 1940s era house. Assembly
techniques were incorporated during the
design to reduce the amount of material.
For its ventilation, the façade is covered
with prefabricated cement panels that
prevent mold and insects.

Site plan

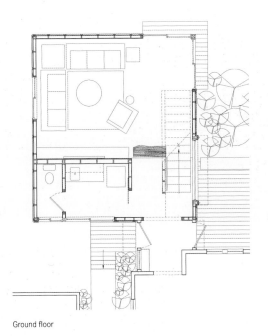

Ground floor

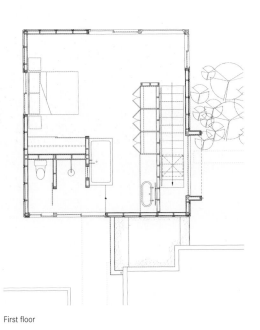

First floor

A polycarbonate panel to one side
of the staircase diffuses natural light
throughout the interior.

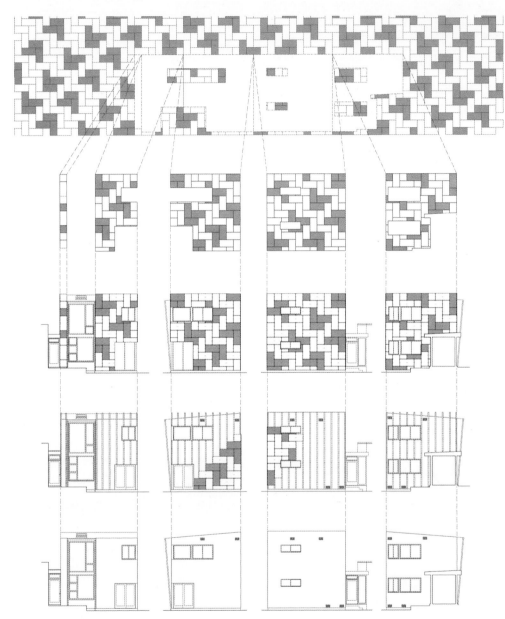

Wrapped cube

MARONAZ HOUSE

La Possession, France

RozO Architectes
www.rozo-archi.fr
© RozO Architectes

1,615 sq ft (150 sq m)
2 bedrooms, 2 washrooms

In situ assembly, steel structure,
concrete panels, polyester and
metal mesh walls

This project's goal is to create a
bio-climatic and ecological house,
adapted to the environment and the
special features of the island. It is a
compact volume, in which the outside
areas, such as the terrace, pool and grill,
are contained within the main volume.
The rectangular plan is laid out over
two levels.

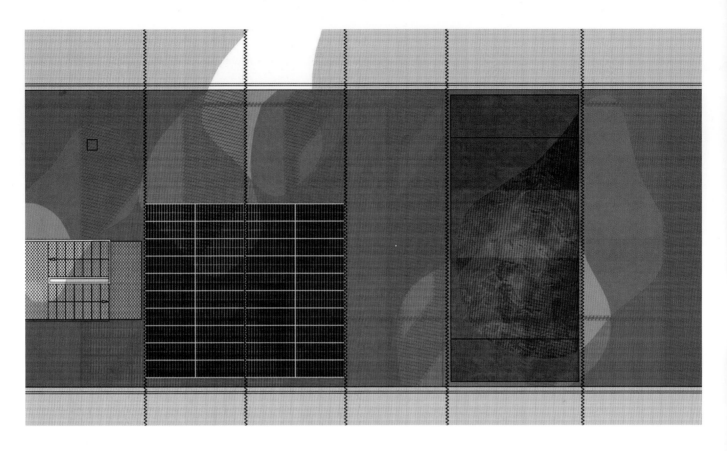

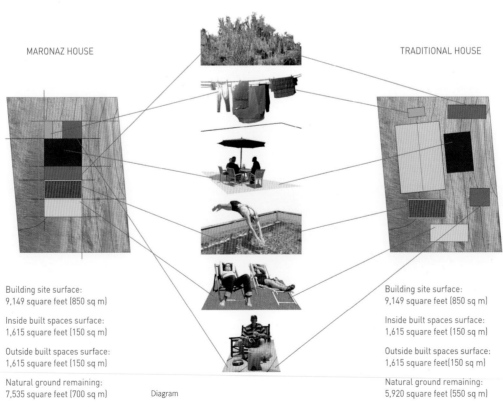

MARONAZ HOUSE   TRADITIONAL HOUSE

Building site surface: Building site surface:
9,149 square feet (850 sq m)   9,149 square feet (850 sq m)

Inside built spaces surface: Inside built spaces surface:
1,615 square feet (150 sq m)   1,615 square feet (150 sq m)

Outside built spaces surface: Outside built spaces surface:
1,615 square feet (150 sq m)   1,615 square feet(150 sq m)

Natural ground remaining: Natural ground remaining:
7,535 square feet (700 sq m)   Diagram   5,920 square feet (550 sq m)

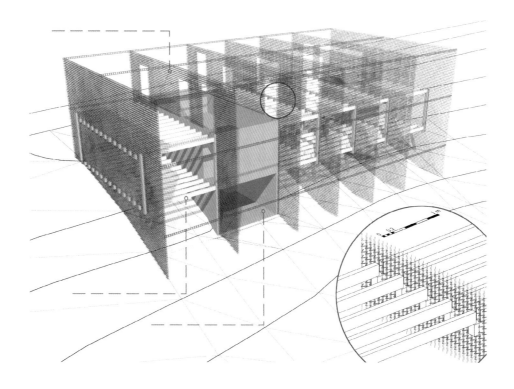

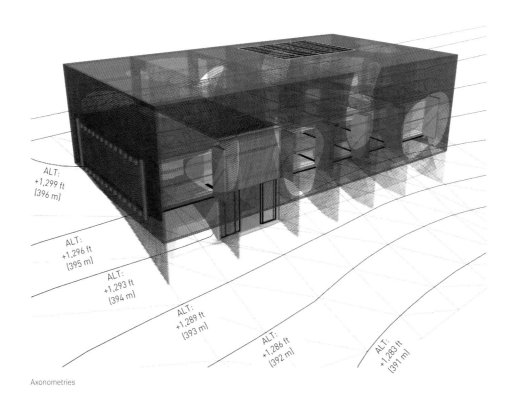

ALT:
+1,299 ft
(396 m)

ALT:
+1,296 ft
(395 m)

ALT:
+1,293 ft
(394 m)

ALT:
+1,289 ft
(393 m)

ALT:
+1,286 ft
(392 m)

ALT:
+1,283 ft
(391 m)

Axonometries

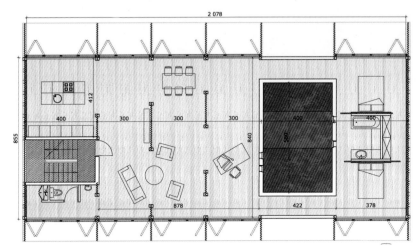

First floor

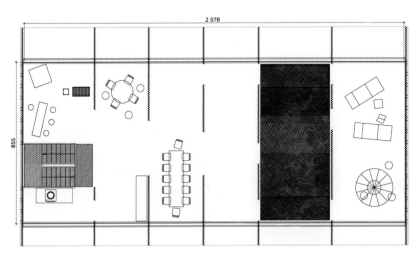

Ground floor

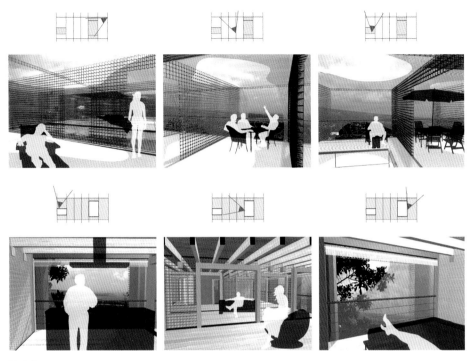

Renderings

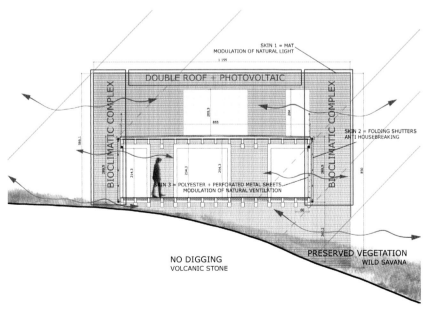

SKIN 1 = MAT
MODULATION OF NATURAL LIGHT

DOUBLE ROOF + PHOTOVOLTAIC

BIOCLIMATIC COMPLEX

BIOCLIMATIC COMPLEX

SKIN 2 = FOLDING SHUTTERS
ANTI HOUSEBREAKING

SKIN 3 = POLYESTER + PERFORATED METAL SHEETS
MODULATION OF NATURAL VENTILATION

NO DIGGING
VOLCANIC STONE

PRESERVED VEGETATION
WILD SAVANA

Bioclimatic diagram

An algorithm has been applied to the house's design so that the windows frame the best views.

PALMS RESIDENCE

Venice, California, USA

Marmol Radziner Prefab
www.marmolradzinerprefab.com
© David Lena

2,800 sq ft (260 sq m)
3 bedrooms, 3 washrooms

Factory pre-assembled modules,
in situ assembly, recycled steel
structure, metal and cedar wood
paneling, CaesarStone and MDF
furniture

This house consists of 14 modules
and 2 levels. The house incorporates
many eco-friendly features, such as
a recyclable steel structure and SIPs,
which reduce heating requirements
by 12 to 14 percent. Triple pane glass
and natural materials reinforce this
component.

The home is completed in less than 7 months: 3 months of factory assembly, 2 months of on-site installation and 6 weeks for finishes and landscaping.

First floor

Ground floor

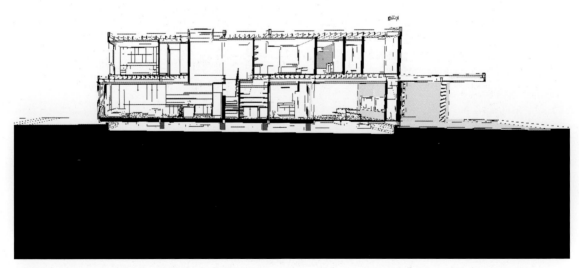

Section

Drawings

SANTA MONICA
PREFAB

Santa Monica, California, USA

Office of Mobile Design
by Jennifer Siegal
www.designmobile.com
© Laura Hull

2,330 sq ft (216 sq m)
2 bedrooms, 3 washrooms

Factory pre-assembled modules,
in situ assembly, fiber cement
siding, aluminum metalwork,
VOC-free paints, bamboo flooring

This house was constructed in the
factory and then assembled in situ
to reduce costs and CO_2 emissions.
Recycled materials such as aluminum
were used in the exterior metalwork, and
low emission glass was used to maintain
the temperature inside the house.

Unlike materials such as stucco and wood, these façade panels are durable and require little maintenance.

First floor

Ground floor

BURGHALDE

Liestal, Switzerland

Stalder & Buol Architektur
www.stalderbuol.ch
© Leo Buol

1,830 sq ft (170 sq m)
3 bedrooms, 2 washrooms

Factory pre-assembled parts,
in situ assembly, metal structure
on concrete blocks, wood panels

This complex consists of 4 semidetached
houses. All the elements of each module
were built at the factory, transported
to the site and assembled quickly. The
austere, neutral design is aimed to
convey a sense of the carefree, and all
materials used are low-maintenance.

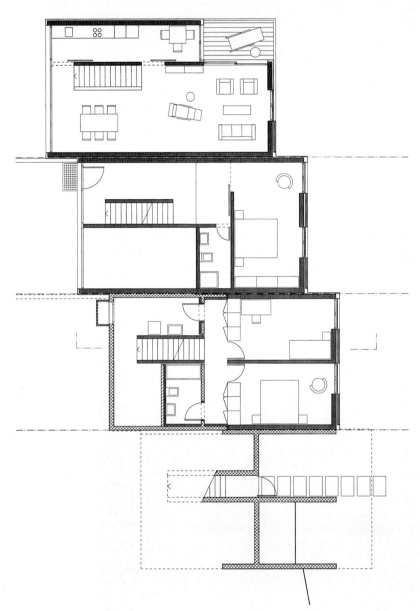

Floor plans

The structure and interior finishes combine traditional and contemporary techniques.

RESIDENTIAL CONTAINERS

Prague, Czech Republic

Petr Hájek Architekti
www.hajekarchitekti.cz
© Ester Havlova

1,625 sq ft (151 sq m)
1 bedroom, 1 washroom

In situ assembly, steel shipping
containers, sheet glass, wood
finishes and metal

Two containers have been placed on
the roof to create the extension for this
home. The living areas were reallocated
to this new top floor, while the original
space is now used for the bedrooms.
An electronic system controls the
natural light entering the interior
and regulates temperature with the
movement of the awnings.

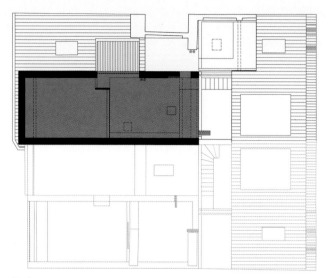

First floor

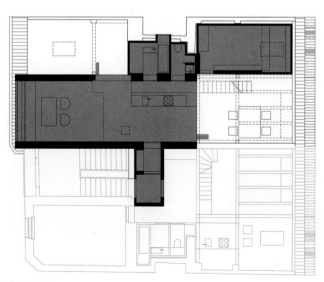

Ground floor

The house has two connected levels. The lack of interior dividing walls allows light to stabilize the indoor temperature.

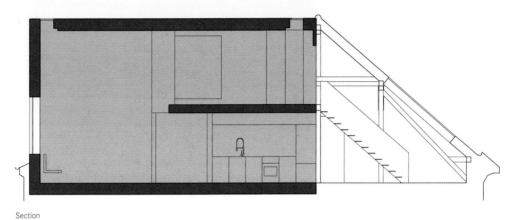

Section

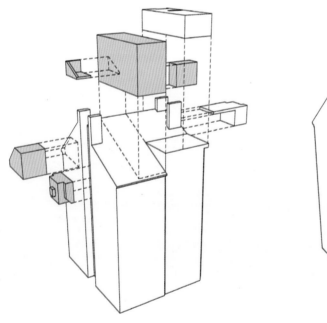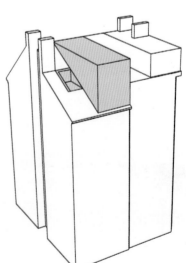

Axonometries

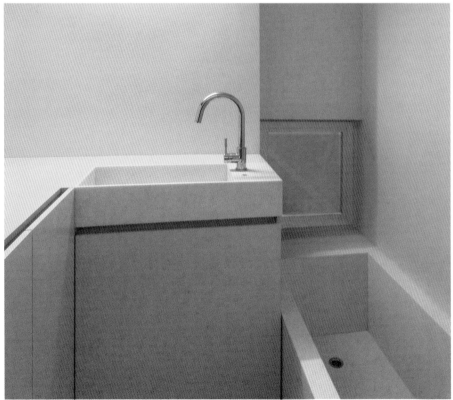

ADRIANCE HOUSE / 12 CONTAINER HOUSE

Blue Hill, Maine, USA

Adam Kalkin/Architecture
and Hygiene
www.architectureandhygiene.com
© Peter Aaron/ESTO

In situ assembly, steel shipping
containers, galvanized steel roof,
glass panels

4,004 sq ft (372 sq m)
4 bedrooms, 3 washrooms

The house has a rectangular floor plan
with two wings, six containers on the
first floor and six on the second. The
rooms are arranged around a central
courtyard paved with concrete; from
there, two staircases lead to private
spaces on the second floor.

The roof is made from galvanized
steel and a skylight above each
staircase allows natural light to enter.

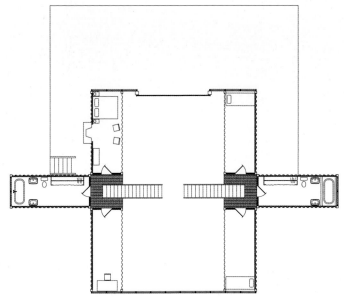

First floor

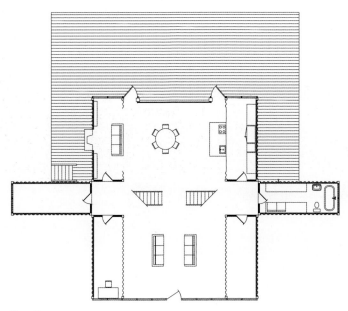

Ground floor

TWO FAMILY HOUSE

Andelsbuch, Austria

Oskar Leo Kaufmann & Albert Rüf, Bmst Johannes Kaufmann
www.olkruf.com
© Ignacio Martínez

Factory pre-assembled parts, in situ assembly, wood panels and frames

3,498 sq ft (325 sq m)
2 bedrooms, 1 washroom

This house consists of two independent units for two families, one on each floor. The layout for each level is distinct, having been configured according to the family's specific needs. There are 10 different types of façade available for selection.

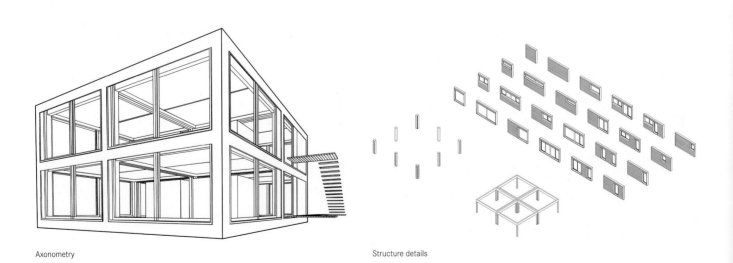

Axonometry

Structure details

Section

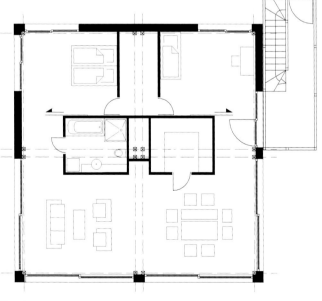

Floor plan

All interior space is distributed
around the kitchen and washroom,
which are located in the center
of the house.

ZEROHOUSE

Suitable for any location

Scott Specht
www.spechtharpman.com
© Devin Keyes, Frank Farkash,
Scott Specht

Factory pre-assembled modules,
in situ assembly, rolled steel
frame, SIPs with exterior covering

650 sq ft (60 sq m)
1 bedroom, 1 washroom

This home is designed to operate
autonomously. It is entirely off-grid.
The home is powered by a battery
network; it collects rainwater and
treats its own waste. The parts of
the home are transported to the site
and are assembled in two days. It
can be installed anywhere, even in
protected areas.

The design is composed of two overlapping rectangular volumes, which separates the living area from the bedroom.

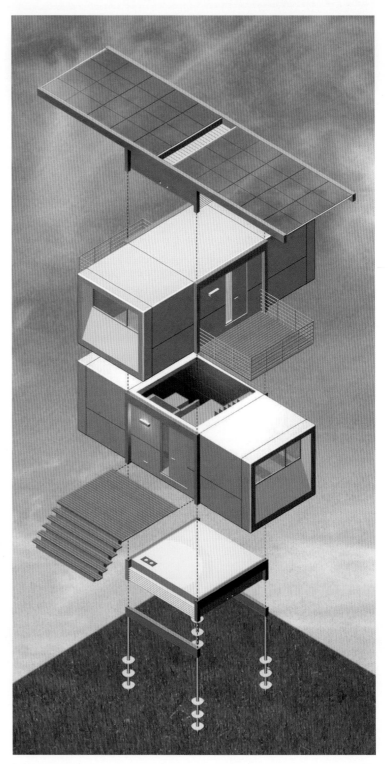

Exploded axonometry

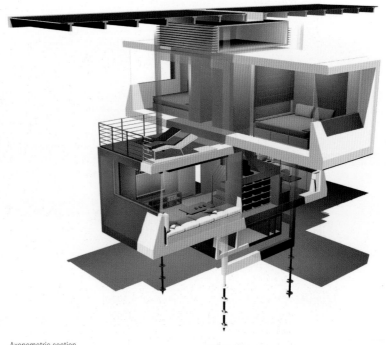

Axonometric section

G HOUSE

Graz, Austria

Gangoly & Kristiner Architekten
www.gangoly.at
© Paul Ott

In situ assembly, prefabricated
metal structure, glass and metal
panels, wood floors and stairs

1,238 sq ft (115 sq m)
1 bedroom, 1 washroom

The ceiling, mezzanine and glass
façades are supported by a system
of prefabricated frames, placed on
the longitudinal axis. In this way, you
achieve an open-plan interior space
with no other structural elements. The
structural materials blend in with the
interior finishes.

The arrangement of the elements of the façade was designed to be harmonious with the arrangement of the home's interior.

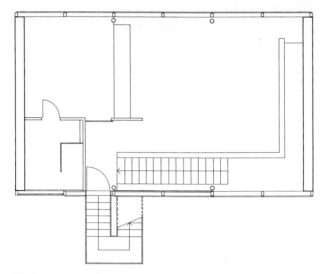

First floor

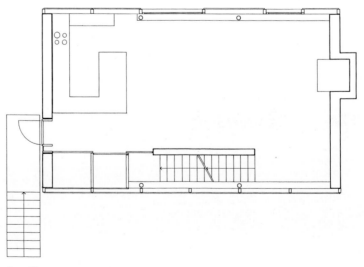

Ground floor

Directory

AFRICA

ECO-BUILDING SYSTEMS NIGERIA
Plot 14A Grace Anjous Drive,
Off Road 14, Lekki Phase 1,
Lagos, Nigeria
+234 1 271 0914
+234 1 812 5402
+234 1 270 6571
www.ecobuildingnigeria.com
info@ecobuildingnigeria.com
* manufacture

ECOMO
+27 72 445 9373
www.ecomohome.com
info@ecomohome.com
* pre-designed houses and manufacture

FSM
P.O. Box 393, Germiston 1400,
South Africa
+27 11 873 0890
+27 11 873 4761
www.fsm.co.za
sales@fsm.co.za
* manufacture

KATE OTTEN ARCHITECTS
28a Sixth Avenue, Parktown North,
Johannesburg 2196, South Africa
+27 11 880 3764
+27 86 648 4875
www.kateottenarchitects.com
kateo@iafrica.com
* architects

KOFFI & DIABATÉ
Cocody Danga Nord, Boulevard
Latrille, 17 BP 59 Abidjan 17,
Côte d'Ivoire
+22 522 48 33 33
+22 522 48 33 34
www.koffi-diabate.com
info@koffi-diabate.com
* architects

MOLADI
P.O. Box 16553, Emerald Hill,
6011 Port Elizabeth, South Africa
+27 41 372 2152
www.moladi.net
mail@moladi.com
* manufacture and construction

NOMC
236 Church Street, Bloemfontein,
South Africa
+27 51 434 2371
+27 51 435 4948
www.noversea.co.za
noversea@lantic.net
* manufacture and construction

**NYUMBA MOBILE HOMES
AND OFFICES**
P.O. Box 25964, Monument Park,
0105 Pretoria, South Africa
+27 83 270 0555
+37 86 544 6529
www.nyumba.co.za
info@nyumba.co.za
* manufacture and construction

ZENKAYA
+258 823 03 28 56 Mozambique
www.zenkaya.com
zenkayablu@gmail.com
* pre-designed houses

THE AMERICAS

@6 ARCHITECTURE
290 Division, Suite 303
San Francisco, CA 94103, USA
+1 415 503 0555
+1 415 503 0550
www.at-six.com
info@at-six.com

ACORN DECK HOUSE COMPANY
852 Main Street, Acton,
MA 01720, USA
+1 800 727 3325
+1 978 263 6800
www.deckhouse.com
* design and construction

ARCHITECTURE AND HYGIENE
www.architectureandhygiene.com
sonofderrida@aol.com
* design

BENSONWOOD HOMES
6 Blackjack Crossing, Walpole,
NH 03608, USA
+1 877 203 3562
+1 603 756 3600
www.bensonwood.com
info@bensonwood.com
* design and construction

BERCY CHEN STUDIO
1111 E. 11th Street Suite 200,
Austin, TX 78702, USA
+1 512 481 0092
www.bcarc.com
info@bcarc.com
* architects

BLU HOMES
760 Main Street, Waltham,
MA 02451, USA
+1 617 275 2333
www.bluhomes.com
* design and construction

BUILDSENSE
600 Foster Street, Durham,
NC 2770, USA
+1 919 667 0404
www.buildsense.com
crew@buildsense.com
* design and construction

CASAS EN BAMBÚ GUADUA
Avenida Ambalá, Conjunto Balcones
de Navarra, Bloque 5, N° 301,
Ibagué, Colombia
bambuguadua.tripod.com
mariofau@yahoo.com
* design, manufacture and construction

CLAYTON HOMES
www.claytonhomes.com
+1 800 822 0633
* design and construction

CLEARSPACE MODULAR HOMES
4801 S. Congress Ave. E4,
Austin, TX 78745, USA
+1 512 663 1962
www.clearspacehomes.com
info@clearspacehomes.com
* design

CLEVERHOMES
665 Third Street, Suite 400,
San Francisco, CA 94107, USA
+1 415 344 0808
www.cleverhomes.net
info@cleverhomes.net
* design and construction

D'ARCY JONES DESIGN
204 - 175 East Broadway,
Vancouver BC, V5T 1W2, Canada
+1 604 669 2235
+1 604 669 2231
www.darcyjones.com
mail@darcyjones.com
* architects

DEMARIA DESIGN
1728 Pico Boulevard,
Los Angeles, CA 90015, USA
1726 Manhattan Beach Boulevard,
Studio J, Manhattan Beach,
CA 90266, USA
20 Park Place, Suite 309,
Morristown, NJ 07960, USA
+1 310 802 1270
+1 310 802 1260
+1 973 829 1920
+1 310 829 1873
www.demariadesign.com
* architects

DESIGN STUDIO MODERN
Box 684742, Austin, TX 78768, USA
+1 512 619 6962
www.designstudiomodern.typepad.com
msmeyer@designstudiomodern.com
* design

EPOCH HOMES
P.O. Box 235, 107 Sheep Davis Road
(Route 106), Pembroke, NH 03275,
USA
+1 603 225 3907
+1 603 225 8329
+1 877 463 7624
www.epochhomes.com
sales@epochhomes.com
* design, manufacture and construction

FABPREFAB
MODERNIST PREFAB DWELLINGS
www.fabprefab.com
* information resource

FLATPAK
+1 612 788 5355 USA
www.flatpakhouse.com
info@lazofoffice.com
* prefabricated components

**FLOAT Architectural
Research and Design**
+1 541 868 6074 USA
www.floatwork.com
erin@floatwork.com
* architects

FORM&FOREST
+1 866 977 3676 USA
+1 866 697 1822 USA
www.formandforest.com
info@formandforest.com
* design and manufacture

GAUTHIER ARCHITECTS
465 Grand Street, 5th floor
penthouse, New York, NY 10002, USA
+1 212 673 2600
+1 212 673 2633
www.gauthierarchitects.com
info@gauthierarchitects.com
* architects

GREEN HORIZON
540 Fillmore,
San Francisco, CA 94117, USA
+1 800 466 8193
www.greenhorizonmfg.com
* manufacture

GREEN MODERN KITS
www.greenmodernkits.com
* design and manufacture

HIVE MODULAR
211 Street Anthony Pkwy, Suite 104,
Minneapolis, MN 55418, USA
+1 612 379 4382
+1 612 331 4638
www.hivemodular.com
info@hivemodular.com
* pre-designed houses and manufacture

I-BEAM DESIGN
245 West 29th Street, Suite 501A,
New York, NY 10001, USA
+1 212 244 7596
+1 212 244 7597
www.i-beamdesign.com
* architects

INFINISKI
Los Conquistadores, 2782,
Providencia, Santiago de Chile, Chile
+56 9 6607 1991
www.infiniski.cl
info@infiniski.com
* design and construction

IT HOUSE
1570 La Baig Ave, Unit A,
Los Angeles, CA 90028, USA
+1 213 380 1060
www.tkithouse.com
* design and manufacture

JAMES&MAU
Ruta 68, Fundo Monterrey, Curacaví,
Región Metropolitana, Chile
+56 9 8790 9743
www.jamesandmau.com
* architects

KIT LOG CABINS
www.kitlogcabins.com
submissions@kitlogcabins.com
info@kitlogcabins.com
* directory

KITHAUS
Los Angeles, CA, USA
+1 310 889 7137
San Francisco, CA, USA
+1 415 816 0579
www.kithaus.com
** pre-designed houses, manufacture
and construction*

**LOGICAL HOMES
LIGHT + SPACE RESOLVED**
www.logicalhomes.com
* design and construction

MARMOL RADZINER PREFAB
12210 Nebraska Avenue,
Los Angeles, CA 90025, USA
+1 310 689 0089
www.marmolradzinerprefab.com
sales@marmolradzinerprefab.com
** custom designed and pre-designed
houses*

METHOD HOMES
3123 Fairview Ave. E, Suite A2,
Seattle, WA 98102, USA
+1 206 789 5553
www.methodhomes.net
info@methodhomes.net
* design and manufacture

**MICHAEL P. JOHNSON
DESIGN STUDIO**
P.O. Box 4058, Cave Creek,
AZ 85327, USA
+1 480 488 2691
+1 480 488 1656
www.mpjstudio.com
michael@mpjstudio.com
* architects

MODULAR DWELLINGS
Edgar Blazona
2729 Acton Street, Berkeley,
CA 94702, USA
www.modulardwellings.com
edgar@modulardwellings.com
* design

MODULAR TODAY
www.modulartoday.com
* consumer reviews

MORPHOSIS ARCHITECTS
3440 Wesley Street, Culver City,
CA 90232, USA
153 West 27th Street, Suite 1200,
New York, NY 10001, USA
+1 424 258 6200
+1 212 675 1100
www.morphosis.com
studio@morphosis.net
* architects

**NEIL M. DENARI ARCHITECTS
(NMDA)**
11914 Washington Boulevard,
Los Angeles, CA 90066, USA
18 West 18th Street, New York,
NY 10011, USA
+1 310 390 3033
+1 310 390 9810
+1 212 652 9127
www.denari.co
info@denari.co
* architects

**OFFICE OF MOBILE DESIGN
BY JENNIFER SIEGAL**
1725 Abbot Kinney Blvd,
Venice, CA 90291, USA
+1 310 439 1129
+1 310 745 0439
www.designmobile.com
info@designmobile.com
* design and construction

PHILIPPE BARRIERE COLLECTIVE
www.philippebarrierecollective.com
philippebarrierecollective@gmail.com
* architects

PIECEHOMES
www.piecehomes.com
info@piecehomes.com
** custom designed and pre-designed
houses*

PRAIRIEMOD
www.prairiemod.com
mail@prairiemod.com
* online community

PREFAB COSM
prefabcosm.com
scott@prefabcosm.com
* information resource

PREFAB HOMES. MODULAR HOMES
www.prefabs.com
submissions@prefabs.com
info@prefabs.com
* directory

QUIK BUILD
59-65 Mine Brook Road, Bernardsville,
NJ 07924, USA
www.quik-build.com
* pre-designed houses and manufacture

RESOLUTION: 4 ARCHITECTURE
150 West 28th Street, Suite 1902,
New York, NY 10001, USA
+1 212 675 9266
+1 212 206 0944
www.re4a.com
info@re4a.com
* architects

ROCIO ROMERO
4579 Laclede Avenue, #132,
St. Louis, MO 63108, USA
+1 314 367 2500
+1 314 367 2505
www.rocioromero.com
* design and manufacture

SCOTT SPECHT
338 West 39th Street, 10th Floor,
New York, NY 10018, USA
1314 Rosewood Avenue, Suite 103,
Austin, TX 78702, USA
+1 212 239 1150
+1 512 382 7938
www.spechtharpman.com
info@spechtharpman.com
* architects

SYSTEM ARCHITECTS
124 West 30th Street, Studio 319,
New York, NY 10001, USA
+1 212 625 0005
+1 800 796 4152
www.systemarchitects.net
system@systemarchitects.com
* architects

TAALMAN KOCH ARCHITECTURE
1570 La Baig Ave., Unit A,
Los Angeles, CA 90028, USA
+1 213 380 1060
www.taalmankoch.com
info@taalmankoch.com
* architects

**TALIESIN / FRANK LLOYD WRIGHT
SCHOOL OF ARCHITECTURE**
P.O. Box 4430, Scottsdale,
AZ 85261-4430, USA
+1 608 588 4770
www.taliesin.edu
nikita@taliesin.edu
* university

TAYLOR SMYTH ARCHITECTS
245 Davenport Road, Suite 300,
Toronto, ON, M5R 1K1, Canada
+1 416 968 6688
+1 416 968 7728
www.taylorsmyth.com
mtaylor@taylorsmyth.com
* architects

**UCLA / ARCHITECTURE
AND URBAN DESIGN**
Box 951467, 1317 Perloff Hall,
Los Angeles, CA 90095-1467, USA
+1 310 825 7857
+1 310 825 8959
www.aud.ucla.edu
admissions@aud.ucla.edu
* university

UNIVERSITY OF ILLINOIS
332-C 1304 W Pennsylvania Ave.,
Urbana, IL 61801, USA
www.solardecathlon.illinois.edu
solardecathlon@uiuc.edu
* university

WEEHOUSE
856 Raymond Ave., Suite G,
St. Paul, MN 55114, USA
+1 651 647 6650
www.weehouse.com
info@weehouses.com
* custom designed and pre-designed
houses, and manufacture

**ZEROHOUSE
LIVE (COMFORTABLY) ANYWHERE**
+1 512 382 7938
www.zerohouse.net/wordpress
zerohouse@zerohouse.net
* pre-designed house

ZUARQ
Kr. 43A, Nº 22-42, Bogotá, Colombia
+57 1481 02 18
www.zuarq.com
info@zuarq.com
* architects

ASIA + OCEANIA

ANDREW MAYNARD ARCHITECTS
551 Brunswick Street, North Fitzroy,
Melbourne, 3068 Victoria, Australia
+61 3 9481 5110
+61 3 8640 0439
www.maynardarchitects.com
info@maynardarchitects.com
* architects

ATELIER TEKUTO
301-6-15-16 Honkomagome,
Bunkyo-ku, Tokyo 113-0021, Japan
+81 3 5940 2770
+81 3 5940 2780
www.tekuto.com
info@tekuto.com
* architects

BACH KIT
200 Fendalton Road, Christchurch,
New Zealand
www.bachkit.co.nz
info@bachkit.co.nz
* pre-designed houses, manufacture
and construction

BALI WOODWORLD
Br. Sigaran, Badung – Abiansemal,
Desa Sedang, Jl. Kamboja 26,
Bali 80216, Indonesia
+62 361 780 18 19
www.baliwoodworks.com
contact@baliwoodworld.com
* design and manufacture

BARK DESIGN PTY LTD
P.O. Box 1355, Noosa Heads,
4567 Queensland, Australia
Studio 185 Sunrise Road, Tinbeerwah,
4563 Queensland, Australia
+617 5471 0340
+617 5471 0343
www.barkdesign.com.au
info@barkdesign.com.au
* architects

**BEIJING CHENGDONG
INTERNATIONAL MODULAR
HOUSING**
6 South Street, Songzhuang,
Tongzhou, Beijing 101118, China
+86 10 6959 7336
+86 10 6959 7331
+86 10 6959 0950
www.globalsources.com/cdph.co
* manufacture

BEIJING JHT STEEL
20 Yuchang Road, Yufa Town,
Daxing District, Beijing, China
+86 10 8757 6284
+86 139 1015 1173
+86 10 8757 6348
www.jhsteelchina.com
* manufacture

CLIMA
RM 3A07, YinGu Plaza, 9 West Road,
North Fourth Ring Road, Beijing
100080, China
+86 10 6280 0700
+86 10 6280 0290
www.fabricated-house.org.cn
wangweiji@clima.org.cn
* manufacture and construction

HUF HAUS
Beijing Zhongguancun Life Science
Park, Beiqing Street, Haidian District,
102206 Beijing, China
+86 135 1103 8030
www.huf-haus.com
beijing@huf-haus.com
* design, manufacture and construction

MODABODE
3 Rosedale Avenue, Fairlight,
New South Wales 2094, Australia
+614 3196 1520
www.modabode.com.au
info@modebode.com.au
* pre-designed houses and manufacture

PREBUILT
219 Colchester Road, Kilsyth,
Victoria 3137, Australia
+613 9761 5544
+613 9761 5572
www.prebuilt.com.au
info@prebuilt.com.au
* pre-designed houses, manufacture
and construction

SMARTSHAX
P.O. Box 272, Avalon Beach,
New South Wales 2107, Australia
+614 1222 3944
www.smartshax.com.au
uptonbuilding@bigpond.com
* pre-designed houses and manufacture

SUPER FAB. PREFAB & DÉCOR
P.O. Box 6737, Sharjah,
United Arab Emirates
+97 16 534 3555
+91 16 534 3636
www.superfab.ae
info@superfab.ae
* manufacture

WARO KISHI
4F Yutaka Bldg., 366 Karigane-cho,
Nakagyo-ku, Kyoto 604-8115, Japan
www.k-associates.com
mail@k-associates.com
* architects

YAODA
N° 20-24, 2nd stair, Block 14,
1 KuiQi Road, (International Metals
Trading Center), Lanshi Town, Foshan,
Guangdong, China
+86 757 8270 6933
+86 757 8270 0609
www.yaodaprefab.com
export@yaodaprefab.com
* design, manufacture and construction

ZHEJIANG XINYUAN COLOR STEEL
Tongji North Road and Gongping
Road intersection, West Lake District,
Sandun Town, 310030 Hangzhou City,
China
+86 571 8889 8000
xycg@xy-cg.com
www.xy-cg.com
* design, manufacture and construction

EUROPE

ABS
av. Conde de Romanones, 22,
Polígono Industrial Miralcampo,
19200 Azuqueca de Henares,
Guadalajara, Spain
+34 902 18 11 06
+34 94 926 46 25
www.abs.es
info@abs.es
* pre-designed houses and manufacture

AMCHALETS
+34 637 84 47 79
www.amchalets.com
info@amchalets.com
* pre-designed houses and manufacture

ARCHITEKTURBÜRO REINBERG
Lindengasse 39/10,
A-1070 Vienna, Austria
+43 1 524 82 80
+43 1 524 82 80-15
www.reinberg.net
architekt@reinberg.net
* architects

ARCHITEKTURBÜRO WALLNER
Zentnerstraße 1, 80798 Munich,
Germany
+49 89 127 00 555
+49 89 127 00 557
www.wallner-architekten.de
info@wallner-architekten.de
* architects

ARQUIMA
av. Guatemala, 10, Local Izq.,
08740 Sant Andreu de la Barca,
Barcelona, Spain
+34 93 682 10 06
+34 93 682 59 74
www.arquima.net
info@arquima.net
* custom designed and pre-designed
houses, and manufacture

BIK VAN DER POL
Tamboerstraat 9, 3034 PT Rotterdam,
the Netherlands
+31 10 402 94 861
www.bikvanderpol.net
info@bikvanderpol.net
* artists

BLOC HOUSE
Ausiàs March, 6-8, Local 2,
08800 Vilanova i la Geltrú,
Barcelona, Spain
+34 93 814 90 60
www.theblochouse.com
info@theblochouse.com
* custom designed and pre-designed
houses, and construction

CASAS MASTER – LERCASA
ctra. Madrid-Irún, km. 203,7,
apdo. Postal 22, 09340 Lerma,
Burgos, Spain
+34 94 717 70 00
+34 94 717 09 69
www.lercasa.com
info@lercasa.com
* pre-designed houses and manufacture

CASAS NATURA
av. Comarques País Valencià, 34,
Polígono Industrial Ciudad Mudeco,
46930 Quart de Poblet,
Valencia, Spain
+34 96 145 28 17
+34 615 11 42 67
+34 657 39 88 15
+34 96 145 25 63
www.casasnatura.com
info@casasnatura.com
* design, manufacture and construction

CASAS PREFABRICADAS VT
Catalunya, 54, Local A,
08225 Terrassa, Barcelona, Spain
+34 93 735 81 90
www.casasprefabricadasvt.com
casas@casasprefabricadasvt.com
* manufacture

CASASTAR GLOBAL BUILDING
av. de las Cortes Valencianas, 39,
bajo 4, 46015 Horta de Valencia,
Valencia, Spain
+34 902 00 66 58
+34 96 193 75 57
www.casastar.es
casastarglobal@gmail.com
* custom designed and pre-designed
houses, and manufacture

CLG CHALETS
+34 902 36 77 84
+34 97 285 64 32
www.clgchalets.com
info@clgeng.com
* manufacture and construction

DAAM
16-24 Underwood Street,
London N1 7JQ, United Kingdom
+44 20 7490 3520
www.daam.co.uk
info@daam.co.uk
* architects

DORTE MANDRUP ARKITEKTER
nørrebrogade 66D, 1.Sal,
DK-2200 Copenhagen N, Denmark
+45 3393 7350
www.dortemandrup.dk
info@dortemandrup.dk
* architects

ECOSISTEMA URBANO
Estanislao Figueras, 6,
28008 Madrid, Spain
+34 91 559 16 01
www.ecosistemaurbano.com
info@ecosistemaurbano.com
* architects

ECOSPACE
3 Iliffe Yard, London, SE17 3QA,
United Kingdom
+44 20 7703 4004
+44 20 7708 4750
www.ecospacestudios.com
info@ecospacestudios.com
* design, manufacture and construction

EKSJÖHUS
Box 255, 575 23 Eksjö, Sweden
+46 381 383 00
www.eksjohus.se
info@eksjohus.se
* manufacture

ELK
Strkovská 297, Planá nad Lužnicí,
391 11 Czech Republic
www.elk.cz
elk@elk.cz
* manufacture and construction

EUROCASA
Merindad de Sotoscueva, 8,
Polígono Industrial Villalonquejar,
09001 Burgos, Spain
+34 94 747 30 74
+34 94 747 32 76
www.eurocasas.com
comercial@eurocasas.com
* pre-designed houses and manufacture

**GANGOLY & KRISTINER
ARCHITEKTEN**
Am Kai, Körösistraße 9,
8010 Graz, Austria
+43 316 71 75 50
+43 316 71 75 50-6
www.gangoly.at
office@gangoly.at
* architects

GRIFFNERHAUS
Gewerbestraße 3,
9112 Griffen, Austria
+43 423 32 23 70
+43 423 32 23 75
www.griffner.com
info@griffner.com
* custom designed and pre-designed
houses, and manufacture

HAAS
Industriestraße 8,
D-84326 Falkenberg, Sweden
+46 872 71 80
+46 872 71 85 93
www.haas-fertighaus.de
falkenberg@haas-fertighaus.de
* pre-designed houses and manufacture

HANGAR DESIGN GROUP
www.hangar.it
hdg@hangar.it
* design

HAUS FINLAND
ctra. de la Coruña, km. 27,250,
28290 Las Rozas, Madrid, Spain
+34 91 630 42 62
+34 91 630 13 21
www.hausfinland.com
hausfinland@hotmail.com
* pre-designed houses and manufacture

HOLZ BOX
Colingasse 3, A-6020 Innsbruck,
Austria
+43 512 56 14 78
+43 512 56 14 78-55
www.holzbox.at
mailbox@holzbox.at
* architects

HOOBY A.
Gnaz-Härtl-Straße 9,
5020 Salzburg, Austria
+43 664 64 11 52
+43 662 64 19 93
www.hobby-a.at
hobby.a@subnet.at
* architects

IBERIA HOUSE
Polígono Industrial Raco,
Carrer de Ponent S/N,
46612 Corbera, Valencia, Spain
+34 96 111 22 24
+34 670 58 38 62
www.casaseuropeas.es
info@casaseuropeas.es
* design and manufacture

INFINISKI
Cava Baja, 47, 28005 Madrid, Spain
+34 628 17 21 39
+34 655 77 10 79
+34 91 366 68 61
www.infiniski.com/world
info@infiniski.com
* architecture and construction

ISOBOX
54 Aigialeias, 15125 Athens, Greece
+30 210 610 88 80
+30 210 610 88 81
www.isobox.gr
* manufacture

KAGER ITALY
Via Calestani 6,
29017 Fiorenzula d'Arda, Italy
+39 523 98 10 06
+39 523 24 08 47
www.kager-italia.it
info@kager-italia.it
* manufacture and construction

KAGER SLOVENIA
Ob Dravi 4a, 2251 Ptuj, Slovenia
+386 2 788 93 10
+386 2 788 93 20
www.kager-hisa.si
info@kager-hisa.si
* manufacture and construction

**KARMOD. PREFABRICATED
TECHNOLOGIES**
E-5 Karayolu Üzeri Aydıntepe
Mah.G.13 Sokak 12 Tuzla,
Istanbul, Turkey
+90 506 918 19 47
+90 216 392 20 45
+90 216 392 80 14
export@karmod.com
www.karmod.eu
* manufacture and construction

**KORTEKNIE STUHLMACHER
ARCHITECTEN**
Postbus 25012, 3001 HA Rotterdam,
the Netherlands
+31 10 425 94 41
+31 10 466 51 55
www.kortekniestuhlmacher.nl
mail@kortekniestuhlmacher.nl
* architects

LE VILLE PLUS
Via Udine 8/A, 33010 Cassacco, Italy
+39 432 85 21 10
+39 432 85 33 71
www.levilleplus.it
info@levilleplus.it
* design, manufacture and construction

LEGNO HOME
Vicolo IV Novembre 2,
32021 Agordo, Italy
+39 340 702 92 93
www.legnohome.it
* manufacture

LITHOUSE
Deltuvos 39c, Deltuvos, Ukmerg
Vilniaus reg., 20126 Lithuania
+370 68 82 98 98
www.lithouse.lt
vaida@lithouse.lt
* design, manufacture and construction

MARTERERMOOSMANN
Grinzinger Allee 50-52,
1190 Vienna, Austria
+43 1 328 92 70
www.marterermoosmann.com
office@marterermoosmann.com
* architects

METALLUMINIO
Via Camozzi, 84, 24100 Bergamo, Italy
+39 35 24 39 13
www.metalluminiocasette.com
metalluminiotrade@gmail.com
* pre-designed houses and manufacture

NOMADHOME
www.nomadhome.com
* pre-designed modular system

OLGGA ARCHITECTES
14, Rue Atlas, 75019 Paris, France
7 ter Bd Louis 14, 59800 Lille, France
+33 1 42 40 08 25
+33 1 42 40 08 59
+33 3 20 52 96 10
+33 3 62 02 16 96
www.olgga.fr
* architects

**OSKAR LEO KAUFMANN
& ALBERT RÜF**
Steinebach 3, 6850 Dornbirn, Austria
+43 5572 39 49 69
+43 5572 39 49 69 - 20
www.olkruf.com
office@olkruf.com
* architects

PAES
ctra. A-62, km. 99,8,
34210 Dueñas, Palencia, Spain
+34 97 976 14 44
+34 97 976 14 45
www.paes.grupoonix.com
paes@grupoonix.com
* manufacture

PANEL CONFORT HOUSE
Urbanización Valdearenas 9,
50300 Calatayud, Spain
+34 97 688 14 74
www.panelconforthouse.com
* pre-designed houses and manufacture

PETR HÁJEK ARCHITEKTI
Grafická 20, 150 00 Prague 5,
Czech Republic
+420 233 35 44 17
www.hajekarchitekti.cz
hajek@hsharchitekti.cz
* architects

PREFABRIK YAPICO INC.
E - 5 Karayolu Üzeri Egemen Sokak
No: 7 34903 Güzelyalı, Pendik,
Istanbul, Turkey
+90 216 392 12 89
+90 216 392 00 64
+90 216 392 21 29
+90 216 392 21 23
www.prefabrikyapi.com
* manufacture

PROVICSA
Polígono Industrial Los Frailes,
Parcela 36, 28814 Daganzo de Arriba,
Madrid, Spain
+34 902 43 17 04
www.provicsa.com
* pre-designed houses and manufacture

QUERKRAFT ARCHITECTS
Mariahilfer Strasse 51,
1060 Vienna, Austria
+43 1 548 77 11
+43 1 548 77 11-44
www.querkraft.at
office@querkraft.at
* architects

RENSCH HAUS
Mottener Str. 13, D-36148 Kalbach,
Rhön, Germany
+49 974 29 10
+49 974 29 11 74
www.rensch-haus.com
info@rensch-haus.com
* design, manufacture and construction

**RINTALA EGGERTSSON
ARCHITECTS**
Stavangergata 46a,
0467 Oslo, Norway
Hyttebakken 33, 8011 Bodø, Norway
+47 22 23 00 06
+47 22 23 00 07
+47 90 51 90 05
www.rintalaeggertsson.com
sami@ri-eg.com
* architects

ROZO ARCHITECTES
2 rue Chapon, 93300 Aubervilliers,
France
+33 950 03 69 01
+33 148 33 03 46
www.rozo-archi.fr
info@rozo-archi.com
* architects

SOFTROOM ARCHITECTS
3 Murphy Street, London SE1 7FP,
United Kingdom
+44 20 3597 6888
www.softroom.com
softroom@softroom.com
* architects

SPACEBOX
Frambozenweg 59, 2321 KA Leiden,
the Netherlands
P.O. Box 841, 2501 CV The Hague,
the Netherlands
+31 61 550 54 14
+31 84 225 24 66
www.spacebox.nl
info@spacebox.nl
* pre-designed houses and manufacture

STALDER & BUOL ARCHITEKTUR
Neugasse 6, 8005 Zurich, Switzerland
+41 44 446 40 50
+41 44 446 40 51
www.stalderbuol.ch
kontakt@stalderbuol.ch
* architects

STUDIO MAKKINK & BEY
Postbus 909, 3000 AX Rotterdam,
the Netherlands
Overschieseweg 52 a,
3044 EG Rotterdam, the Netherlands
+31 10 425 87 92
+31 10 425 94 37
www.studiomakkinkbey.nl
studio@jurgenbey.nl
* furniture design

TECTONIKS
Unit 1, Kinton Business Park,
Nesscliffe, Shrewsbury, Shropshire
SY4 1AZ, United Kingdom
+44 17 43 74 11 99
+44 17 43 74 16 34
www.tectoniks.com
info@tectoniks.com
* design and manufacture

VIVNATUR
ctra. N-I, km. 20800,
28709 San Sebastián de los Reyes,
Madrid, Spain
+34 91 651 65 21
www.vivnatur.com
info@vivnatur.com
* pre-designed houses and manufacture

WOLFGANG FEYFERLIK
Glacisstraße 7, 8010 Graz, Austria
+43 316 34 76 56
+43 316 38 60 29
* architects

WOLFHAUS
Zona Industriale 1,
I-39040 Campo di Trens, Italy
+39 472 06 40 00
+39 472 06 49 00
www.wolfhaus.it
* design, manufacture and construction

Date Due

MAR 2 2 2015			
OCT 0 7 2015			